Hurst, Euless, and Bedford

Heart of the Metroplex
An Illustrated History

by George N. Green

EAKIN PRESS ★ Austin, Texas

FIRST EDITION

Published in the United States of America
By Eakin Press
An Imprint of Sunbelt Media, Inc.
P.O. Drawer 90159   ★   Austin, TX 78709-0159

2   3   4   5   6   7   8   9   0

ISBN 0-89015-951-3

Library of Congress Cataloging-in-Publication Data

Green, George N. (George Norris)
    Hurst, Euless, and Bedford : heart of the metroplex : an illustrated history / by George N. Green. — 1st ed.
        p.   cm.
    Includes bibliographical references and index.
    ISBN 0-89015-951-3
    1. Hurst (Tex.) — History. 2. Euless (Tex.) — History. 3. Bedford (Tex.) — History. 4. Hurst (Tex.) — Pictorial works. 5. Euless (Tex.) — Pictorial works. 6. Bedford (Tex.) — Pictorial works. I. Title.
F394.H94G743   1995
976.4'531–dc20   94-24113

                                      CIP

Contents

Preface

The writing of the history of Hurst, Euless, and Bedford involved the help and cooperation of many people. I am greatly indebted to Dee Barker, Duane Gage, and Weldon Cannon for reading chapters of the manuscript and offering necessary corrections. Harold Samuels and Dodie Souder were also helpful on the last chapter.

Various institutions and individuals provided valuable assistance with their files. The Tarrant County Historical Commission and the Heritage Room of the Tarrant County Junior College Library have preserved much of the history of the area. Professor Duane Gage initially gathered many of the records housed at TCJC, where the collection is maintained by Paul Davidson, while Dee Barker and her staff preside with much hospitality at the Historical Commission. Very useful clippings files are kept at the tri-cities libraries by Betty Yarborough and her staff in Euless, Bonnie Finn and the staff in Bedford, and Evelyn Hatcher and Danita Barber and the staff in Hurst. The unheralded research and writings of Tex Adams, Duane Gage, and Michael Patterson were treasured sources, as were the preservationist efforts of Evelyn Fitch-George, Gordon Doggett, Betty Fuller, Arlene Sturm, and Dodie Souder. The HEB school district, the HEB Chamber of Commerce, the Dallas and Fort Forth public libraries, and my old friends in Special Collections at the University of Texas at Arlington Library were also very cooperative. The most delightful part of the project was interviewing dozens of HEB residents, most of whom are getting along in years, and all of whom were keenly interested in recollecting past events. They are too numerous to name, but I remember them all and applaud their commitment to the community.

Most of the photographs were selected by Professor Gage from the holdings in the Heritage Room. Gage also wrote most of the accompanying captions. Troy Fuller, Jean Whitener, and the Euless Historical Preservation Society were instrumental in providing many of the Euless photos. Evelyn Fitch-George, Hattie Bell Cribbs, and Dodie Souder contributed several Bedford and Hurst photographs. I thank them all for their generosity and their counsel.

Finally, I am grateful for the understanding and patience of my family, who bore with me throughout this undertaking. This book is for them — Kathy, Valerie, and Deanna Green.

I. Exploration and Settlement, to 1880

From Prehistory to the Texas Frontier

In ancient times the Southwest was covered by a warm, shallow sea. Silty deposits buried many of the marine animals as they perished and preserved them through fossilization. Fossilized sharks' teeth are among the common remains deposited in the mid-cities area. Seventy to ninety million years ago one of the larger denizens of the North Texas sea was the plesiosaur, a twenty-five foot long, ten thousand-pound reptile with a crocodilian mouth and flippers. In 1972 the fossilized skeleton of one of these behemoths was uncovered during construction of a drainage ditch on the Dallas-Fort Worth Airport site. Paleontologists meticulously restored the plesiosaur, which is now on permanent display on the third floor of the airport's central utilities plant. The creature is older than the Rocky Mountains, which were thrust upward about sixty million years ago. As the land rose, the fragments of the sea drained rapidly into the Gulf of Mexico. The future site of Tarrant County thus sloped from over a thousand feet in the northwest to less than five hundred in the southeast.

A half-million years ago huge mastodons, twenty-five feet tall and covered with heavy hair, roamed the North Texas area and shared the Trinity basin with early varieties of camels and horses as well as bison and mammoths. The bison remained, but the other animals were supplanted by speedy jackrabbits, wolves, coyotes, deer, and antelope. The eventual site of Tarrant County lay at a juncture of a warm, humid eastern zone and a semi-arid western region. The Black Prairie on the eastern edge of the county comprised a rolling grassland of rich, black soil, attractive to grazing animals. From an aerial view one can see the contrast between the Black Prairie, on which the Dallas-Fort Worth Airport was built, and the sandy, wooded Eastern Cross Timbers (including much of Bedford and Hurst). Forests of blackjack and post oaks prevail, the remnants of which survive today at a few sites, such as in and around Rickel Park in southeastern Hurst. Within the county are at least twelve rivers and creeks. The Clear Fork and the West Fork of the Trinity River drain the western half of the county, while most of the tributaries, such as Big Bear, Little Bear and Walker creeks, flow into the Trinity in the eastern half.

The ancestors of the American Indians first reached North America by migrating across the Bering Strait when a land bridge connected the continents, some 20,000 years ago. These prehistoric hunters may have been ancestors of the Caddo Indians, a major woodland culture indigenous to north central and northeast Texas. Between the Black Prairie and the Eastern Cross Timbers, old Minter's Chapel Road on the airport grounds followed the natural game and Indian trails. Caddo and other Indian campsites have been found along the margin between these two geographic regions and elsewhere in the upper Trinity basin. As early as a thousand years ago the Caddos built permanent villages with large circular houses and raised corn, squash, beans, and pumpkins and maintained orchards of peach and plum trees. They also hunted on the prairies and in the glades of the Cross Timbers. Many travelers considered the Caddos peculiar because they practiced cra-

Prehistoric. Evidence that Northeast Tarrant County was once significantly populated by the Caddos and related tribes is found in literally bushels of arrowheads and other relics collected at sites in the area.

– Courtesy Tarrant County Junior College

nial deformation in an effort to elongate the bone structure, and because they cried and moaned when greeting newcomers.

The Caddos and other eastern woodland tribes co-existed and sometimes conflicted with the Plains Indians, where they met around the three forks of the Trinity. During the eighteenth century the elaborately tatooed plains tribes of the Wichita Confederacy (Wacos and Tawakonis) abandoned Kansas and became the most numerous folk occupying the headwaters of the Trinity basin. They too were a semi-agricultural people, who hunted buffalo on horseback, but relied considerably on gardening. They built large villages comprised of grass thatched, log houses. During the eighteenth century the aggressive Apaches pushed the Comanches and Kiowas, noted for their painted faces and horned headdresses, from their plains hunting territories to the upper Trinity lands of the Wichitas, where they forged a tenuous alliance against the Apaches. All the plains and woodland tribes left behind various place names in the Southwest as well as thousands of arrowheads, knives, drills, and bowls in the mid-cities area alone.

In 1714 French trappers founded the trading post of Natchitoches on the Red River in Louisiana. The French traveled to Indian settlements as far west as the forks of the Trinity, exchanging trinkets and knives for pelts, hides, and horses. But the Spanish, with their base in Mexico, maintained a stronger control over Texas. Ironically, Spanish rule was symbolized by an expedition headed by a Frenchman, Athanase de Mezieres y Clugny, to the upper Trinity in 1778. De Mezieres, former lieutenant governor of Lousiana, accepted citizenship and a frontier command from the Spanish. De Mezieres' reports described the clear Trinity River abounding in fish, the lush river valley and wooded groves, the fertile prairies of grass and wild grapes, and the astounding amount of game. He noted that the numerous creeks and springs could be used for irrigation and the timber for building materials if Spain could develop the region. He visited and surveyed the tribes, and hoped to hold their allegiance against the possible future incursion of English traders from their American colony. Even as he maneuvered, however, the American Revolution was setting free the former colonists for a westward movement that was destined to overwhelm the Hispanic outposts in Texas in the nineteenth century.

In the 1790s Philip Nolen, an American adventurer who was in contact with Vice-President Thomas Jefferson, secured permission from Spanish authorities to hunt wild mustangs in Texas. Operating between present Waco and Fort Worth, Nolen and his men rounded up wild horses and herded them to Natchez and other towns in the southern United States, where hundreds were sold. Nolen lived with Texas Indians for a time, then resumed his horse trading operations in 1801, but the Spanish became suspicious of his activities and killed him and some of his men at his corral. Other Americans helped weaken Spanish rule through armed filibustering expeditions in Texas in the early 1800s. Mexico, then including Texas and the American Southwest, won her independence from Spain in 1821.

Mexico promptly allowed American Catholics who would accept Mexican citizenship to settle in Texas. Hailing mostly from the border southern states, lured by free and fertile land, some thirty thousand Americans had located in

1840s. The stockaded walls of Bird's Fort have disappeared and the site almost destroyed by gravel excavations. Its construction was similar to this replica of Fort Parker near Mexia, Texas, where in 1836 a white child, Cynthia Ann Parker, was abducted by Indians. – Courtesy *Fort Worth Star-Telegram.*

Texas by the mid-1830s. No Anglos, however, were tempted to colonize the Indian-"infested" lands of the upper Trinity. The Texas Revolution freed the settlers from Mexican rule, but the Republic of Texas, 1836–1845, was often plagued by Indian attacks, as both plains and woodland tribes grew restive over the Anglo encroachment on land they regarded as theirs.

The first known Anglo-American expedition into present Tarrant County occurred in 1838, when some ninety Northeast Texas frontiersmen waged a punitive raid against Indians who had attacked their homes in Fannin County. Led by Captains Robert Sloan and Nathaniel Journey, they overran a small village and killed several Indians in the vicinity of present-day southern Euless, probably at the present site of the Arlington landfill. A Texas Historical Marker just south of Euless on State Highway 157 notes the event. After clashes on Village Creek in present Arlington in the spring of 1841, Capt. Jonathan Bird, an Alabama veteran of the Texas Revolution and a resi-

dent of Bowie County, asked Texas Militia Gen. Edward H. Tarrant if he (Bird) could establish an outpost on the Trinity River. Tarrant agreed. The fort would form the nucleus of a civilian colony and furnish protection against hostile Indians. Most Caddos and Wichitas migrated to the west and north, opening up the Trinity basin for tentative settlement. With about thirty-five volunteer Rangers, Bird chose a site inside the curve of a crescent-shaped lake (later named Lake Calloway) on the north side of the Trinity River, one-half mile south of the present intersection of Calloway Cemetery Road and South Main, south of the present Euless city limits. They erected a tall blockhouse and several cabins, three of which were enclosed in a stockade.

The country was regarded as having great potential, one prospective settler remarking, ". . . it is the best range country I ever saw to raise stock . . ." But the Indians had burned off all the grass in the surrounding country and no game was to be found; all supplies had to be hauled from present

Bonham at Bird's personal expense. The Rangers and several families that had joined the encampment were soon destitute of provisions and during one week had nothing to eat; they were saved by eating some discarded calves' bones, which they boiled. One settler, hunting for bears, was ambushed and killed by Indians.

This first recorded Anglo occupation of present Tarrant County lasted only three months. The people had been confident that they would receive free land under the Republic's Military Road Act, but it was superseded by the 1841 Peters Colony contract and ensuing legislation that extended colony land south to include the area of the fort. The settlers were so informed in February 1842. Bird wrote his congressman, ". . . my little band was refused protection by the agent of the colony, therefore with great dissatisfaction, and aggravated mortification, the fort was vacated." According to General Tarrant, the fort was "in the limits granted to Browning and others."

Downstream about twenty-two miles to the east, John Neely Bryan, a young Tennessean, had been recruiting settlers for his new village since 1840 and had helped build Bird's Fort. He revisited the fort at about the time of the Peters Colony news — possibly it was Bryan who brought the word — and invited the remaining survivors to move to the fertile lands near him. Disenchanted by the malarial conditions and thoroughly discouraged by the Peters Colony encroachment, some followed Bryan while others returned to their homes in East Texas. Since the Peters Colony also included Bryan's area, following him did not necessarily resolve problems in claiming land. Those who agreed to settle near Bryan's homestead reputedly asked him to name the place; Bryan may have named it for a friend named Dallas. Another of several versions, however, credits a refugee from the fort — Capt. Mabel Gilbert's wife, Charity — with the naming of the settlement. Bird's Fort remained in sporadic service for about ten years.

Meanwhile, the financially desperate Republic of Texas promoted a policy of robbery. President Sam Houston and the Texas Congress authorized Jacob Snively to lead an expedition northward and seize Mexican freight trains as they passed along the Santa Fe Trail to and from Missouri, across territory claimed by Texas. Snively and seventy-six men ran head-on into a 200-man U.S. Cavalry force, which disarmed the Texans and forced their humiliating retreat to Bird's Fort. There they disbanded on August 6, 1843.

That same month President Houston journeyed to Bird's Fort to attempt a council of peace, under the full moon, with all the Texas tribes. The northern frontier, he thought, "bled at every pore with Indian depredations and treachery." Arrayed in a purple velvet suit, with a huge Bowie knife thrust in his belt, Houston promised the chiefs of the ten tribes represented that an inviolate treaty line should be drawn with trading houses (including one near the confluence of the Clear Fork and the West Fork of the Trinity) established along it. He waited impatiently for the Comanches, while one British adventurer noted in his diary, "After spending several days at the swampy fort, Houston withdrew in a rage to the higher ground at Grapevine Springs. There he fretted for almost a month before returning to Washington on the Brazos." Houston left George Terrell and General Tarrant to conclude negotiations as soon as the Comanches arrived. Finally on September 29, 1843, the Bird's Fort Treaty line was agreed to, extending from the hunting grounds north of the West Fork of the Trinity to present Menard and San Antonio. The irate Comanches never appeared, but placing their marks on the document were the chiefs of the Caddo, Tawakoni, Waco, and seven other tribes. Most of the Indians in North Texas remained northwest of the treaty line, so the upper Trinity became peaceful and the farming-ranching frontier was thrust westward in the 1840s. A Texas Historical Marker, just south of Euless on State Highway 157, commemorates the site of the fort, which has now been virtually surrounded by sand and gravel excavation.

Beginning in 1843, immigrants, mostly from Tennessee and the rest of the border South, began trickling into the upper Trinity region. The soil was rich, the water and game abundant, the forests and wildflowers attractive. Uneasy about its shaky finances and volatile relations with Mexico and the Plains Indians, the Republic of Texas actively attempted to lure settlers to the new nation. Through the impresario system, immigration agents contracted to colonize a certain number of families within a specific area and prescribed time period. The first arrangement was made with W. S. Peters and Associates (from Louisville, Kentucky, and London, England), who agreed in 1841 to bring 600 families into the colony within three years. The Peters Colony was a strip of territory whose boundaries shifted several times, but it soon stretched 100 miles long in

North Central Texas and over 160 miles wide south of the Red River. It included present Tarrant, Dallas, and twenty-one other counties. White family men were eligible for a section (640 acres) and single men 320 acres. To obtain clear title to the free land the immigrants had to live on it three years, cultivate at least ten acres, and have the land surveyed and plainly marked. For each 100 families settled, the company was to receive ten premium sections of land. The Republic and the company disputed ownership of various tracts, while many immigrants settled inadvertantly on company land. Also, speculators received land to which they were not entitled. Land titles became confused and years of litigation followed, though most land claims were adjusted in the 1850s.

Nobody can identify with certainty the first permanent settler in Tarrant County. Within the present county, somewhere along the Trinity around 1843, two Arkansas trappers, Edward S. Terrell and John P. Lusk, attempted to establish a log cabin trading post. Indians seized them and held them captive for almost a year. They left the state and returned in 1849. By 1845 farmers were settling along creeks in the northeastern area of the county. Several families, notably the Crowleys, located near the juncture of the Little Bear and Big Bear creeks on property now owned by the Dallas-Fort Worth Airport. Their spokesman was Isham Crowley (1798–1878) from Virginia by way of Alabama and Missouri. He and his large family settled on a Peters Colony survey of 640 acres. The creek was supposedly named for another early settler Daniel Barcroft. "Bear" was generally pronounced "bar" by Southerners at that time and perhaps his name was associated with "Dan'l killed a bar." Along present West Hurst Boulevard, considered part of the Birdville community at the time, Hamilton Bennett also filed on 640 acres and built a cabin there. He was a Church of Christ preacher from Virginia via Missouri; he left Tarrant County in 1858. By 1848 settlers were also established in Birdville on Big Fossil Creek, part of present Haltom City, ten miles west of the old fort. Indeed, by 1848, the last year of the Peters Colony contract, dozens of families had settled in the area. Besides Bennett and Crowley, those who actually settled within present HEB through 1848 included Solomon Haworth, Allen Trimble, Samuel Tucker, Patrick Everard, Sanders Elliot, Abraham Bernard, Andrew Huitt, and

M. W. Wilmeth. Bennett and Barcroft served as county commissioners for a time.

John Hust (1811–1868) settled on a tract, roughly between Walker Branch and the Trinity, between 1846 and 1848. He patented 640 acres in 1854, shortly before he and three partners built a grain mill on Hust's land. The mill was erected on the south bank of the Trinity, about a hundred yards west of the present Precinct Line Road bridge. "Leonard's Mill," named for primary owner Archibald Leonard, was propelled by a turbine motor, which turned the water wheel and ground the grain. It became an industrial center for the North Texas area.

In 1845 the Republic of Texas voluntarily joined the United States, and the annexation was a primary cause of the war with Mexico, 1846–1848. In January 1849 Maj. General William Jenkins Worth, a hero of the war and an officer risen from the ranks, was given 1,000 men, about a tenth of the U.S. Army, to protect the 500-mile Texas frontier plus several hundred more miles along the Rio Grande. He set out to build a line of ten forts. Bvt. Maj. Ripley Arnold and forty dragoons established the northern fort on a bluff on the West Fork of the Trinity, June 6, 1849. General Worth died of cholera in San Antonio, and Arnold named his site Fort Worth. The post included cabins, a sawmill, and a hospital; its parade ground was the current courthouse square. Tarrant County, with an area of about 860 square miles, was carved out of Navarro County later that year and named for Gen. Edward Tarrant. The largest, centrally located village, Birdville, was selected as the county seat by popular vote in the first election, August 5, 1850. The 1850 census revealed 664 county inhabitants, including sixty-five slaves, but 15 or 20 percent of the total population was probably missed by the government. The majority undoubtedly lived in the northeast quadrant of the county.

The fort, on the easily defensible high bluff, held the primary responsibility for the defense of the growing villages and farms along the upper Trinity. By this time, visiting Indians came mostly to trade or carouse, but the blue-uniformed dragoons fought two successful skirmishes with the Comanches, 1849–1850. The army deactivated the base in 1853 due to the rapid westward movement of the Texas frontier. The settlers took possession of the site, converting every building into civilian establishments.

During the first two or three years these immigrants from the border South and the Midwest had to be supplied by ox wagon from Shreveport, Louisiana. The first settlers in the 1840s lived mainly on honey, venison, wild turkey, bear, and buffalo meat, but their diet soon shifted toward cornbread, bacon, beef, butter, and coffee. Flour was a luxury few could afford. Men's and boy's clothing — coats, pants, leggings, and moccasins — were crafted from buckskin and deer sinew, but spinning wheels and hand looms were soon utilized. Pioneer women spun and carded their cotton and wool, and wove it into jeans and cotton fabrics from which they made their clothing. Clothes were also purchased in such places as Jefferson in East Texas.

The great majority of settlers were farmers, of course, raising corn, grain, cotton, and cattle, but there was also a goodly number of merchants, blacksmiths, preachers, doctors, and others among the early arrivals. The land was cultivated by plows drawn by oxen. Grains were cut with a cradle and threshed by primitive machinery. The great event of winter was "hog killin' time," accomplished with a thrust at the jugular vein with a sharp butcher knife. Much of the carcass would be consigned to the smokehouse, where it was rubbed with saltpeter and hung up so that the smoke from a hickory chip fire smouldered under it for three weeks. When it was thoroughly cured, it was stored away for future use.

Diversions from the humdrum of rural and village daily life, 1840s–1860s, included church socials, quilting parties, singing bees, spelling contests, corn shuckings, candy-pullings, and dances. One pioneer, Howard W. Peak of Fort Worth, recalled years later that, "Coon and possum hunting was a sport for moonlight nights, and the bay of the hound and the hunter's horn could be heard in every vale . . ." Children hung their Christmas stockings by a real fireplace; the chimney was large enough to admit Saint Nick.

Nine offspring of John Hust and Hamilton Bennett, along with twenty other students, comprised the District 14 School, probably located near the present southern city boundary of Hurst. The pupils were listed among the free whites, ages six to sixteen, in the 1854 Tarrant County School Census.

Among the first permanent settlers in present Euless were Alexander Dobkins and his wife Mary, who left Tennessee with their children and came to Texas in 1852. Ensconced on 200 acres within the bounds of the present Dallas-Fort Worth Airport, near the confluence of Big Bear and Little Bear creeks, Dobkins helped organize the Bear Creek Baptist Church in 1853 and Center Spring Baptist in Birdville in 1856. The Bear Creek congregation first met in the home of Isham and Elizabeth Medlin Crowley (1799–1878), whose family constituted seven of the nine charter members; the Dobkins' were the other two. Dobkins was ordained by the church in October, 1855 and apparently served as its pastor for over a year. Crowley donated five acres for the Bear Creek Cemetery in the 1850s, located on the east side of the Highway 360 access, part of old Minter's Chapel Road, a third of a mile north of the Harwood intersection.

In 1857 the Crowley and Dobkins clans and new neighbors, such as the Lee Borah and Joseph Jones families, were allowed to establish a U.S. Post Office, which they named Estill's Station. Jefferson Estill (1820–1855) and Benjamin Crowley (1827–1904) were the first two postmasters, 1857–1860, and were succeeded by Dobkins in 1860. Education in Texas was largely consigned to local, private initiative before and during the Civil War. In 1860 Ben Crowley donated land for a church and school, and a building was erected in the vicinity of the cemetery. The Tarrant County School Census of 1854 reveals thirty-five pupils in the Bear Creek School; a Mr. Houge was the teacher until 1869.

Religion, of course, was also a private matter and local tradition holds that the Bear Creek Baptist congregation was uneasy about the possibility of Indian raids and that many were armed as they attended services. The pastor reputedly preached with his six-gun lying on the altar beside the Bible. Church members, however, were expelled if they failed to attend regularly. The Bear Creek/Estill community, stretching eastward from the cemetery area to the county line, also included a store and a cotton gin.

A general store of that era — and it did not change markedly the next several decades — displayed dry goods on one side, e.g. ribbon, thread, corsets, suspenders, neckties, and underwear. Across from these, near the front, would be a section devoted to hard candy in jars, tobacco, cough drops, patent medicines (such as Radway's Ready Relief) and perhaps a stationery section and a few books. Then, on shelves, would be displayed crockery, tableware, washbowls, glasses, lamps, and jugs. Next would come the grocery section with cheeses, a spice grinder, tins of spices, tea, and coffee, boxes of dried fish, and barrels of crackers, sugar, molasses, gin, and cider. At the rear were farming implements — pitchforks, hoes, whetstones, scythes, horsewhips, leather harnesses, and such. Many storekeepers were also postmasters, but this was not the case at Estill's Station.

Birdville, whose outskirts embraced the western edge of present Hurst, gained a famous frontier resident in 1853 when Isaac Parker bought Hamilton Bennett's farm and his cabin, located just beyond the southwest corner of the current Hurst city limits. Parker had served extensively in the congress of the Republic and the state legislature, and his niece, Cynthia Ann, had been kidnapped at the age of nine by the Comanches in 1836. "Parker Valley" stretched south to the Trinity, southeast of where Highway 10 and Loop 820 intersect in present Hurst. Parker's domicile was typical of the better early homes, being a double log cabin separated by an open breezeway. One part was a kitchen, with a fireplace for cooking, and the other section was a living room and sleeping quarters. The logs were notched and caulked, the floors puncheoned, and the roof built of handmade shingles. It is preserved today at Log Cabin Village in Fort Worth. By 1860 Parker had built a two-story home with a large white-columned veranda and an outside stairway leading to the second story. According to local tradition, his wife Lucy believed the new home was too fine to live in and continued to reside in the old cabin until her death in 1867. Parker was a prosperous homesteader and accepted a final seat in the legislature, 1855–1856.

As North and South drifted toward Civil War, a Texas Ranger raid in West Texas rescued a white captive. Cynthia Ann Parker was no longer able to speak English when she and her baby daughter, Prairie Flower, were repatriated in 1860. Cynthia Ann was the "White Queen of the Comanches," married to Chief Peta Nacona, and she did not want to return to American civilization. She lived in Uncle Isaac Parker's cabin for several months, but yearned for the Indian way of life and attempted several escapes. Moved to other relatives in East Texas, where her daughter died, she never adjusted to the Anglo world or to Prairie Flower's death. Nor did she ever again see

ca. 1856. Isaac Parker was a noted state legislator who moved to a Northeast Tarrant County homestead in 1853. He was an uncle of legendary Cynthia Ann Parker, a white captive who had been living with the Indians since her abduction at age nine in 1836. His farm was located near the present IH 820 and State Highway 10 intersection.
– Courtesy Tarrant County Junior College

her eldest son, Quanah, who succeeded his father as chief of the Staked Plains Comanches. She died in 1864.

One of the oldest final resting places in the county is Parker Family Cemetery, located on a hill just north of Highway 10 and east of Loop 820 in present Hurst. Lucy Parker is buried there along with her son Isaac Duke Parker, who was also prominent in Tarrant County as a legislator, wartime county commissioner, and combat veteran. Other members of the family and their slaves are also interred there. Neither Cynthia Ann nor her Uncle Isaac were buried in Parker Cemetery. She was first interred in East Texas, then reburied by Quanah Parker in 1910 near Cache, Oklahoma. Her uncle remarried in 1870 at the age of seventy-seven and moved to Parker County, which was named for him. He is buried near Weatherford.

ca. 1848. Isaac Parker's cabin, built by pioneer Hamilton Bennett about 1848, was well-constructed with notched logs and hand hewn shingles. Now restored in Fort Worth's Log Cabin Village, it is a rare antebellum Tarrant County structure.
– Courtesy Michael E. Patterson

1870s. Samuel Witten's impressive sixteen-room house was one of the first to be constructed of milled wood in Tarrant County. It was located on the north side of present Cheek-Sparger Road, which divides the cities of Bedford and Colleyville.
– Courtesy Tarrant County Junior College

1977. The city boundaries of Hurst, Euless, and Bedford join at historic Arwine Cemetery, now surrounded by homes and apartments adjacent to the Bellaire Shopping Center. Entrance is via Arwine Cemetery Road and Pipeline Road.
– Courtesy Tarrant County Junior College

1981. An official Texas Historical Marker for Spring Garden community is located on the south side of Cheek-Sparger Road in Bedford, at the site of the old community cemetery. Neglected and unprotected by descendants of those buried there, today the Spring Garden Cemetery is the site of suburban homes.
– Courtesy Duane Gage

1984. When the HEB School District opened a new school in north Bedford in 1983, it was named Spring Garden, for the first school in the community. An official Texas Historical Marker was dedicated at the new school's entrance. – Courtesy Duane Gage

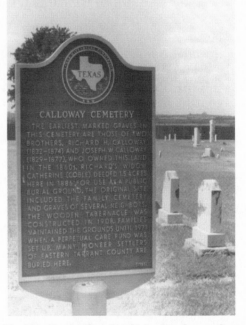

1979. The significance of Bedford Cemetery was recognized with the dedication of this official Texas Historical Marker.
– Courtesy Duane Gage

1991. Used by pioneer families living in the southern part of present Euless, Calloway Cemetery received an official Texas Historical Marker in 1980. – Courtesy Duane Gage

From the Frontier to the Farm, 1860–1880

Just as the Parker family was tragically divided over a captivity, the United States was being torn apart by the presence of over three million captives. Slaves were not numerous in Tarrant County, and some of the county's ablest men supported Gov. Sam Houston's efforts to stave off Texas' secession from the Union. But most border state southerners adhered to their southern ties and on February 23, 1861, the county voted narrowly to secede, while the state approved by a three to one ratio. A half dozen or so companies from Tarrant County rode off to serve the Confederacy in various theaters, while the county's population dwindled from 6,000 to 1,000. The stores ran out of goods, schools closed, and local authorities were forced to issue a county currency. Parched wheat and barley sufficed for coffee, while oil-soaked sycamore balls were used for lighting.

Some post offices closed during the war, but Alexander Dobkins kept his station open in his home, under Confederate authority. He and his daughter handled the present Euless area's mail and that of other nearby settlements until the station was closed by the post office in 1868. Dobkins died in 1869 and became the first person buried in the family plot, which is maintained today on airport grounds and noted with a Texas Historical Marker.

Meanwhile, Samuel Witten (1819–1891), a surveyor and farmer, established a large farm and ranch near Little Bear Creek in present Colleyville before the war. A native Kentuckian, he and his growing family left their home in Spring Garden, Missouri, with two surreys and two covered wagons, and arrived in Tarrant County about 1854. Witten's two-story, sixteen-room house built of milled wood was unique for the time in Tarrant County. He served as the county's deputy surveyor in the 1850s, a Confederate recruiting and supply officer during the war, and a justice of the peace during the Reconstruction years. Witten was generally accepted by other nearby settlers as the guiding spirit of the emerging Spring Garden community, which gained its name and community identity near the end of the war.

Milton Moore (1828–1914), a native North Carolinian, journeyed to Texas from Cole County, Missouri. and brought his family to present Bedford in 1861. He hurriedly built a log cabin in the woods, north of what is now Bedford Road near Barr Drive. He also taught present Bedford's first school in his home in the winter of 1861-1862, and rushed off to join the Confederate Army. The school "year" was only three months long, and the twelve to fifteen students used desks of split logs. Two other teachers taught sessions there the next three winters, but the class quickly outgrew the residence cabin.

Far to the east, the Confederate States of America was crushed in the spring of 1865 by Union armies. The defeated South was prostrate after the war, but Texas and Tarrant County were eventually rejuvenated by southern immigrants. The 1870 census showed almost 5,800 county inhabitants; most were farmers, but there was a growing number of ranchers and businessmen. A few of them were Northerners, but most were Southerners who were determined to start over in a land less ravaged than the rest of the South by

ca. 1865. Samuel S. C. H. Witten arrived in Tarrant County about 1854 and established the Spring Garden community, named for his previous home in Spring Garden, Missouri. He prospered as a land surveyor who was often paid for his services in land. During the Civil War he was a Confederate recruiting and supply officer.

– Courtesy Tarrant County Junior College

the ordeal of the war. A few, like Witten and Moore, already resided in the area and returned from the war determined to get on with their lives.

Early in 1865 Sam Witten suggested to Milton Moore, Caleb Smith, and Levin Moody, all settlers in the Bear Creek and Sulphur Branch watersheds, the possibility of constructing a school. The men readily agreed. Witten took his ox team that he had used as a supply officer and a big load of flour, meal, and bacon — some of which may have been Confederate supplies left in his possession — and made the six-week round trip to the saw mills near the East Texas town of Jefferson, where he swapped the goods for lumber. Moore and the others built the Spring Garden School along present-day Cheek-Sparger Road just northwest of the Spring Garden Cemetery; Witten donated the land for both. Completed in the fall of 1865, the school was a log cabin, fourteen feet square, with a huge fireplace and log-hewn desks and chairs.

For a small country school it had a distinguished faculty. One of the first was Prof. William Hudson, an Englishman who had taught earlier in Birdville and later elsewhere in the county. He eventually joined the faculty at Trinity University in San Antonio. Confederate veteran Cadwell Raines taught for a time and later served as county judge and newspaper publisher in East Texas and finally as director of the Texas State Library around the turn of the century.

Most of the schoolchildren hailed from what later became Colleyville, Bedford and Euless, but some were from Grapevine (then Dunnville) and Birdville and perhaps a few from as far away as Jack and Collin counties. Pupils from outside the community boarded with veteran instructor William Hudson. Milton Moore, the father of several students, plowed a furrow through the woods for two miles from his home to the school. Small children could follow it from Moore's neighborhood as they crossed the post oak forests on their way to and from school. What is now dubbed "continuing education" was carried on also. On one occasion, for instance, a Dr. James Bacon conducted a thirty-five-day "Rapid-Fire Grammar School," attended by fifteen or twenty area teachers as well as Spring Garden residents.

The school building also served as a community meeting site and as a church for members of the Methodist, Church of Christ, and Baptist faiths from about 1865 to around 1872. When a $300 budget was presented for the nine-church Grapevine-Denton circuit in 1870, the Spring Gar-

den Methodists were asked for only ten dollars of the amount. A larger Church of Christ group convened there, served by the eloquent Brother M. G. Elkins. It boasted eighty-one additions in 1868. Four years later the nationally famous church leader David Lipscomb spoke at Spring Garden and denounced Elkins as an adulterer who had left his wife in Tennessee and departed with a prostitute. The amazed congregation immediately discharged Elkins because of unfavorable public opinion. Lipscomb then rebuked the congregation for failing to terminate Elkins on the basis of a Biblical precept.

By this time (1867–1874) congressional Reconstruction in Texas was underway, wherein the victorious U.S. Army occupied the South and former slaves were granted citizenship and the right to vote. Free public schools open to all children

ca. 1870. Dr. Benjamin Franklin Barkley of Birdville opposed secession and openly expressed his pro-Union sentiment during the Civil War, but opened his home to needy families of Confederate soldiers and treated wounded rebels who had been injured fighting against the Union. He was appointed county judge in 1867 after Confederate sympathizers were removed from office. Strongly resented by rebel veterans, he served at considerable risk to his safety. Union soldiers escorted him to the courthouse in Fort Worth and back to his home and medical practice in Birdville each day. – Courtesy Tarrant County Junior College

ca. 1880. Born into slavery in 1827, Robert Johnson became the first black man to live in Mosier Valley, when he married Dilsie, who was given a wedding present of about forty acres by her former masters, the Lees.

– Courtesy Vada Johnson Collection, Tarrant County Junior College

1870s. Occasionally HEB area residents were exposed to the excitement of Fort Worth's wide-open cowtown atmosphere, when business brought them to the county seat. There they could camp overnight in a wagon yard in the square, or in a grove along the Trinity River. – Courtesy Flossie Longley

were mandated by law in 1870 and 1871. Some dissenting white Southerners joined night riding organizations such as the Ku Klux Klan. The forty- or fifty-man Tarrant County organization — some estimates are higher — attempted to intimidate blacks and whites who were part of the Republican Reconstruction process. They whipped several freedmen in Village Creek and Mosier Valley.

After the passage of the Federal Amnesty Act of 1872, most adult, white, male Texans could vote again. The ensuing reaction against Reconstruction was so deep-seated that no Republican won a statewide office until 1961 or a Tarrant County office until 1984.

Adding to the turmoil of Reconstruction was the prohibition against frontier communities from maintaining militias for home defense at a time when Quanah Parker's Comanches and their Kiowa allies were still restless. In the late 1860s these tribes raided Johnson Station (in present Arlington), Blue Mound, and the Marine Creek area, then just north of Fort Worth, but in the mid-1870s they were routed by the U.S. cavalry and Texas Rangers. In 1875 Quanah Parker rode into Fort Sill in Indian Territory and surrendered 400 tribesmen. Dedicating the rest of his life to guiding the Comanches down "the white man's road," he became a successful farmer, rancher, and diplomat for Indians.

Fort Worth was the lively nexus of the county in large part because of a new industry. Texans hit upon the idea of driving large herds of surplus longhorn cattle from the South Texas open ranges to northern markets. One route led through Fort Worth. From the mid-1860s through the mid-1870s "Cowtown" served as a rest and recreation stop and supply point for trail drivers on the way to railroad shipping stations in Kansas. There were many small trails through North Texas that converged north of the Red River such as the Chisholm Trail. Some cattle trailed between Arlington and Grand Prairie through the Bird's Fort area and present Euless in the 1870s.

Some settlers in present HEB were ranchers. From the Bear Creek community, J. E. Fuller later recalled that cattle might be driven for two days to Fort Worth, with an overnight stop near the present location of the Birdville Coliseum. Sam Witten raised cattle and horses, and his oldest son, G. W., survived four years in the Confederate Army, but drowned in 1868 in present-day Oklahoma while driving a herd of cattle from Spring Garden to Kansas.

ca. 1880. Weldon Wiles Bobo (1813–1884) moved from Bedford County, Tennessee, in 1870, built a home, and opened a store, which became the focus of the community that was named after his native county in Tennessee. So many of Bobo's former neighbors and relatives migrated to the area that Bobo pitched a large tent near his store, to accomodate them until they each found homesteads. Soon Bedford had several stores, a gristmill, and a cotton gin.
– Courtesy Tarrant County Junior College

Cowboys as well as area farmers could find considerable gambling, drinking, and prostitution in "Hell's Half Acre" section of Fort Worth along present Commerce Street. Cock fights, dog fights, and occasional shoot-outs were also part of the entertainment. Several stagecoach holdups occurred within the city limits in the 1870s. Area farmers could not avoid the bustling town, since county business was transacted there, and corn and grain could be ground there. If the roads were passable, a farmer's wagon could make a ten mile trek in a day; most visitors would then spend the night in McBride's Wagon Yard.

The great majority of immigrants in the county still made their living by farming. By 1870 Weldon W. Bobo (1813–1884), another Confederate veteran, had emigrated from Bedford County, Tennessee, and established a general store about two miles south of Spring Garden. Located about halfway between Fort Worth and Grapevine, Bobo's Store became a halfway station for travelers to rest. The main street was Bedford

Road, which seems to have begun as a wagon trail to and from Milton Moore's home and Bobo's Store.

Two years or so after their arrival, Bobo and his son began operation of a gristmill that supplied the immediate community with gin and mill service. The mill was propelled by an inclined wheel measuring about forty feet across. The power was produced by the weight of cattle or horses on one side of the wheel. A small settlement grew up around the store and mill, and on one occasion a group of farmers gathered there suggested naming the village "Bobo's Store." Bobo would have none of it and the group then decided on the name "Bedford," after the county in Tennessee from which a number of them had come. (The "Bedford" name dated back to ninth century England, and the Texas village took the identical place name as sixteen other sites in the U.S. and one British dukedom.) Perhaps it was in the early or mid-1870s that government horseback riders from Dallas began delivering the mail to the well-situated store each Thursday, though another account states that by 1877 the mail buggy shuttled from Fort Worth to Birdville to Zion (part of present North Richland Hills) to Bedford to Grapevine and back again. A U.S. Post Office was officially established in Bedford in 1877, and Bobo served a year and a half as first postmaster.

Bedford was already a competing crossroads settlement when Spring Garden was hit with tragedy around 1872. The community building burned. In 1874 Bobo and Milton Moore drove their wagons to the lumber mills of East Texas to fetch building materials for a new church. The new site was on Moore's farm, present 2401 Bedford Road, adjacent to Bobo's Store. Probably the families of Moore, Bobo, Richard T. Valentine (1837-1906), and Wiley Green Cannon (1842-1903) were among the charter members of the church and the construction crew for the new frame building. As in many churches of the time, there were often not enough members for a full-time pastor, so the congregation was frequently served by itinerant preachers. In 1877 Moore sold the five acres of land for $50 to the trustees of what was named the New Hope Christian Church.

Part of the tract included a graveyard that had probably been in use since the 1850s or 1860s. A number of pioneers are buried in the old Bedford Cemetery in unmarked graves. The cemetery was used by members of all faiths. It reached its peak useage in the 1920s and 1930s. There may be as many as 500 people buried there. The cemetery bears a Texas Historical Marker and is located just east of Bedford and Central, next to the Bedford Church of Christ (which succeeded New Hope).

Spring Garden students ceased to meet as a body, though many of them did attend the New Hope School (in the church building) from about 1873 to 1881. Other schools absorbed some of the remaining students.

The southern parts of the Spring Garden community soon became identified as a part of Bedford. The school claimed seventy-three students in the spring of 1877 and eighty-three in the fall of 1881. In 1879 W. A. and Alice Wright were added to the staff to teach eighty or so students. The married couple were remembered for steering the students toward high moral conduct, for holding rigorous reading and arithmetic recitations, and for presiding over Friday afternoon debates for the male students. Math, reading, and spelling were the whole curriculum. Wright was also the preacher in the church about 1879–1880. Former student Lee Hammond remembered that Wright thought teachers had more influence than preachers, which was the subject of a debate with a Presbyterian preacher — the building was filled to capacity on debate night.

Another Bedford school was established by Daniel Glassco, who hailed from Anderson County, Texas. He settled in present East Bedford in 1860, fought in the Confederate Army as a private, and fathered a large family. He founded the school on his property in 1877 in a log building. It sat on the present-day 4200 block of Bedford Road about a thousand feet west of its intersection with State Highway 157 and operated more than twenty years, but few facts about it have survived.

While most of the county's excitement was in Fort Worth, Ed Cromer (1873–1970), born in Bedford, recalled years later what was perhaps HEB's first violent death: "Indian Joe was killed for stealing horses by Doc Cash and Lyle Hugh Newton and was buried on Aunt Sue Smith's NW corner, now Mrs. Dodie Cannon's place." Cromer's parents were from Illinois via Missouri, and his father had been a soldier in the Union Army.

Another early Bedford settler was William Letchworth Hurst (1833–1922), a Confederate veteran who was captured twice during the war and survived over two years in Union prisoner of war camps. Probably after hearing good reports regarding northeast Tarrant County from his old Claiborne County, Tennessee, neighbors he migrated to the area in a two-horse wagon in 1870 with his wife, Mary Ann (Lynch) Hurst and seven children. They lived in present Euless briefly, then moved to Bedford. Their second Bedford home, c. 1876, was a two-story house on the east side of Bedford Road just north of its intersection with present Airport Freeway. They remained there until the late 1890s, while "Billy" raised corn and cotton and speculated in land and Mary sold butter and eggs. One of their sons, Emerson Hurst (c. 1866–1964), reminisced about Bedford in the 1870s, "There wasn't more'n 100 people, just living in log houses here and there. I lived in a log house 13 years. I started to school once — I was about 12. But the little ole girls could outread me. That was downright embarrassing, so I quit and took to dancing."

Other crucial post-war immigrants were the tall, bearded Daniel Arwine (1830–1887) and his wife Julia (1832–1913), who migrated from Indiana in 1865 and settled on a farm centered on the southeast quadrant of the present intersection of Brown Trail and Pipeline in southeast Hurst. Arwine, a Reconstruction Republican, was apparently a deputy U.S. marshal; he would keep prisoners in his home overnight before the long horseback trip to Fort Worth the next day. He built the usual two-roomed log cabin with a breezeway in between and accumulated extensive lands in the present Hurst area.

In 1879 the Arwines' young daughter, Katy, died suddenly, having mentioned earlier that when she died she wanted to be buried under the big tree that she often played beneath. On June 23, 1879, the Arwines deeded six acres to the community for a school, church, and cemetery (where their daughter was already interred).

Traditional accounts state that a one-room school was then built — at first called the Red Sulphur Spring School, named for the spring (and the red dirt) at the foot of the hill that provided drinking water for the community — and that later the school was named for Arwine. It appears, however, that the school preceded the deeding of the land and that both names were used. The *Fort Worth Standard* published a list of county schools in April 1877, listing Arwine with forty-seven students. Other lists revealed Red Sulphur Springs with fifty-one pupils for the 1879–1880 school year and thirty-three in the fall of 1881.

The Arwine Church was evidently not affili-ated with any denomination. The Arwine Cemetery, with nearly 300 identifiable graves, is now a noted historical site, surrounded by homes and apartments next to the Bellaire Shopping Center. This is the only location where the boundaries of present Hurst, Euless, and Bedford join each other; the old cemetery binds the area together geographically as well as historically.

The mists of history are sometimes impenetrable, and little information has survived about the mysterious Male and Female College of the West Fork Baptist Association at Red Sulphur Springs. However, it is recorded that in 1877 A. Fitzgerald, as president and sole agent of the college, bought about two sections for $2,000 from himself, as president and sole agent of the Fort Worth Western Irrigation and Canal Company. Three years later as company president he bought the land and "appurtenances" back from himself as college president for $20,000. Then, acting as guardian for Eva Fitzgerald, he sold half the land to her for $1,000. It is impossible to fully interpret these maneuvers, but one suspects the West Fork Baptists emerged as losers.

In 1878 Jeff Souder (1840–1921), his wife Mary Ellen East Souder, who was Arwine's niece, and several children arrived by train in what was variously called Red Sulphur Springs or the Arwine Community. The Indiana family purchased seventy acres of land south of Arwine's property.

E. E. Souder's family made the trip in 1880 and bought 160 acres, including the property where the Harrison Lane Elementary School now stands. In 1880 or 1881 one or more covered wagon caravans containing the Anderson, Brown, Robertson, and Sexton families also arrived from Indiana. As in the case of the Tennessee clans, the Indiana families had known each other back in the old state and tended to intermarry with each other. The Sexton clan, headed by Enoch (1813-1890) and Sarah Arwine Sexton (1808–1896), journeyed in seventeen wagons and one hack. They circled the wagons at night and occasionally fired into nearby wooded areas to discourage Indian horse thieves.

Over two miles south of Arwine's farm, a Georgia Civil War veteran, the Reverend Marion Isham (1831–1904) established the eleven-person Isham's Chapel congregation around 1876, near Precinct Line and Trammel Davis roads south of the present Hurst city limits. The congregation first met there in a small log schoolhouse or arbor. An acre gift of land for a school and a church was deeded by B. H. Ross in September 1876. Reputedly lumber was hauled by wagon from Eagle Ford near Dallas — described as the nearest railhead at the time — and a frame structure was erected. Perhaps the church is a bit older than the current claim or perhaps the hauling and building began before the land was deeded, since by July 1876, Fort Worth was the nearest railhead. Within the church it was the custom for many years for men to sit on one side of the aisle and women on the other. Eleven students were enrolled in the school in 1879–1880. Marion Isham also established a cemetery, c. 1870, though burials had taken place earlier. It is located at present 7100 John T. White Road in Fort Worth.

Another Tennessean from Bedford County was Elisha Adam Euless (1848–1911), a large man with sideburns, whose mother was Casander Bobo. He journeyed to Tarrant County as a bachelor in 1870. Arriving in Grapevine with the clothes on his back and a $200 draft, he sold the draft for seventy-five cents on the dollar and began a new life on the frontier. In July 1870 he married Julia Trigg (1839–1923), daughter of another Bedford County family. The young couple evidently farmed in the 1870s in Bedford. In 1876 Euless was elected constable of Precinct Three in Tarrant County. In 1880 he made an unsuccessful bid for county sheriff. His defeat did not dampen his enthusiasm, and greater things awaited his career in the 1880s and 1890s.

Other 1870s developments included the arrival of still more pioneers, such as the J. E. Fuller (1858–1936) family from Tennessee. Fuller bought land for $5 an acre in the Bear Creek community, but declined an offer to swap his prize mules for land that is now part of the Dallas-Ft. Worth Airport. The George Morrison family from Georgia settled just north of Little Bear Creek, raising and selling corn, cotton, grain, and melons. Oral tradition holds that during the hard times of the 1870s the present Euless settlement was dubbed "Needmore" and "Hard Scrabble." That decade also saw the arrival of the Grange, a national farmers organization designed to counteract the loneliness and backwardness of farm life through social and educational activities.

A school session was held as early as 1876 in an old one-room building, about twenty-feet by thirty-five-feet, around the northwest corner of present Airport Freeway and Euless Main. Historian Glenn Holden states that there were fifteen or twenty students who were poorly taught. In 1877 the Grangers erected a two-story community hall nearby. They utilized the top floor while the bottom was used as a school and, on alternating Sundays, as a church for the Presbyterians and Methodists. The first teacher, Westard Wallace, was remembered for his classical education and for reciting history as he rode his horse. The second schoolmaster, a Mr. Stewart in 1878–1879, was recollected less fondly because of his "mad fits," free use of the lash, and inability to work all the math lessons. The Bear Creek School still operated on the eastern edge of present Euless, with twenty-seven students in 1877 and twenty-six in 1879. The First Methodist Church was founded in 1876 with about fifty charter members; the first preachers were circuit riders who rode from church to church.

Just south of the present Euless city limits is the Calloway Cemetery, on the 12600 block of Calloway Cemetery Road between State Highway 157 and South Main Street. Probably functioning as a burial ground since the 1860s, it is the final resting place for many of the successful farmers, businessmen, and community leaders — especially those, such as the Calloway family, that emigrated to the area from Bedford, Franklin, and Coffee County, Tennessee.

Over two miles west of Calloway Cemetery another community was established in the early 1870s, long identified as part of present HEB — Mosier Valley. It was founded by eleven emancipated slave families, most of whom had been taken from Tennessee through Missouri to the J. K. or T. W. Mosier plantation on the site of the present Bell Helicopter plant. After being set free with few household possessions and nowhere to go, a number of freedmen and their families died of pneumonia, floods, and illnesses related to poor living conditions. Some black families were given land by Mosier and by the nearby Lee family, whose plantation was about a thousand acres located generally southwest of the current Bell plant. Many freedmen hung on and scrimped and saved in order to purchase this Trinity bottom land, paying anywhere from $1 to $5 an acre. Robert and Dilsie Johnson were the first settlers, accepting a forty-acre tract of land as a wedding gift from the Lees. Miss Lucy Lee also donated two acres to the community for a cemetery. The African Americans established a close-knit farming community named after former owner Mosier. They raised cotton and corn for cash crops, maintained gardens with a variety of vegetables, and kept hogs, cattle, and chickens. A number of them worked as handymen, sharecroppers, farm hands, and nannies for HEB area farmers and villagers.

None of the former slaves could read or write, and they especially wanted to be able to read the Bible. It was probably in the 1870s that they welcomed the arrival of Ellie Cusey or Cursey, a literate black man from Oklahoma. Although an infidel, he agreed to read from the Bible for them and he remained in the area for several years, sharing his knowledge.

A church was established in 1874 that soon took the name of Oak Grove Baptist, but it lacked a permanent site. When weather permitted, the congregation often met in brush arbors. They were served by traveling ministers of different denominations.

Pioneer days were fading by the end of the 1870s. Of all the communities mentioned, only Fort Worth was a town and only Bedford was immediately destined to become a town, but all — as we will see — contributed to the pageant of Tarrant County history.

late 19th century. Bedford pioneer Milton Moore's large family motivated him not only to provide this two-story domicile to house them, but also to help establish local schools. He cofounded the Spring Garden School in 1865, the New Hope School in 1873, and Bedford College in 1882. – Courtesy Tarrant County Junior College

II. Villages and Farms, 1880s–1910s

Settling In, 1880–1900

For about a quarter of a century, beginning in the late 1870s, Bedford was a booming town. By the early 1880s it boasted two cotton gins, two drug stores, three general stores, two blacksmith shops, two saloons, a gristmill for grinding corn into meal, a doctor's office, and a college. Reputedly there were twenty-eight enterprises along Bedford Road, so there was probably also a barbershop, a pool hall, and a restaurant or two. Given the horse culture of the time, a livery and feed store or two would have been likely and perhaps a harness and saddle dealer. The population was between 1,000 and 2,000.

By 1901, when seventeen-year-old G. W. Corbett moved to Bedford, it had slipped considerably. He remembered that there were two stores owned by Richard Valentine and one by Joel Bobo. His father, C. T. Corbett, bought the one remaining blacksmith shop. The one gin he recollected, was owned by John Fitch. There was still no electricity, no gas, no phones, and no plumbing. Householders made do with coal oil lamps, privies in the backyard, and water from cisterns or wells in the backyard or from the well at Bobo's Store. People still visited instead of making telephone calls. The town's leading musician was Will Miller, who always had people bringing instruments to his house and enjoying the frequent playing, singing, and dancing.

Until about the turn of the century, when residents came to town to make purchases and catch up on local news, they usually dropped by to pick up their mail. There were no mail boxes or door-to-door delivery. If the postmaster had a crowd, he would call out the names of people who had mail. During the post office's first twenty-seven years of operation, until the spring of 1904, Richard T. Valentine was postmaster on three occasions for about sixteen and a half years. The post office was in his store at least part of that time. Early in the century John Moore became the first Bedford letter carrier, distributing mail after it was picked up in Arlington.

In 1881 J. H. Smithers and his wife came to Bedford from Thorp Springs and boarded with the Milton Moore family. Mrs. Smithers was allegedly from St. Louis, Missouri, and interested in community affairs. The new couple talked up the benefits of building a school and in 1882 the Moores donated land for Bedford College, a building erected on the site where the historic Bedford Elementary School now stands.

The painted, two-story building was modern for the era, and this private boarding college was the asset that distinguished Bedford from other small communities. The school opening was scheduled for the first Monday in October 1882, but was delayed a week because the stoves did not arrive on time. Stockholders included Moore, Bobo, J. P. Hammond, Green B. Trimble, and others who bought stock and contributed labor. Mrs. Smithers and Alice Wright were hired as instructors for the first year, and J. H. Smithers taught and headed the college, but the Smithers' departed the next year. Something of a combination of high school and junior college, the college offered advanced work in geometry, Latin, algebra, rhetoric, and composition, among other subjects. Music and oratory were added sometime later.

Students were not classified into different grades, and no prescribed course of study was followed.

James A. Clark, who had attended Winchester Normal School in Tennessee, arrived in 1884 and perhaps did more than any other single person to establish a progressive reputation for the school. It even attracted students from out of state. Clark made the college the intellectual and entertainment center for the community, but he moved to Hillsboro after two years.

Several other professors allegedly continued to offer high-caliber instruction, but by 1888 or 1890 it appears that the quality of instruction had waned and that the private "college" had become a public elementary and secondary school. The building burned suddenly in 1893. Many never forgot the night of the fire. Lee Hammond recalled that a man ran down the street shouting, "Bedford College is gone!" A rumor circulated that disgruntled headmaster D. J. Liles had been fired by the trustees and had acted as arsonist. Shortly afterwards, two of the college's former students, Lee Hammond and Marshall Trimble, were the educators who founded Arlington College (1894), the present day University of Texas at Arlington.

Given the hard times that set in with the depression of 1893, the college was not rebuilt immediately. Bedford schooling once more reverted to the New Hope Christian Church, which apparently had been abandoned as a school in the 1880s. To finance a new building, a literary society was organized to put on plays, recitations, and speeches. By about 1896 a new frame building was placed in use and served until 1912. There were eighty students in the fall of 1896 and ninety-five in 1897. The educational offerings in Bedford School District Number 33 continued to be elementary and secondary through the eighth or ninth grades. The Glassco School continued to operate in Bedford and may have served as the public school in the Bedford district during the years that Bedford College was private.

In 1884 Texas passed a law providing for clear separation of private and public educational efforts and for fixed-boundary school districts with elected trustees in each county. During the 1890–1891 school "year," which was four months long, Glassco School District Number 85 was separated from Bedford. The school, which claimed forty-five students in the 1896–1897 year, continued meeting at the Glassco site at Bedford Road and State Farm-to-Market Road 157 until the building burned around 1898. One of the Glassco trustees, William Evatt, donated an acre of his land nearby in 1899, and the Crossroads School began meeting in a new building on the southwest corner of present Airport Freeway and 157. The district was soon named for Evatt.

Few records have survived from Bedford's churches of the time. Harvey Sparger (1833-1914), Confederate veteran from Tennessee and Georgia, led an effort to buy land in present north Bedford in 1886, moved a building there and reconstructed it, and established the Oak Grove Methodist Church. A Baptist church was organized with nine charter members in Bransford in the 1880s, then united with some other small groups, and moved to Bedford.

Many Texas congregations in the nineteenth and early twentieth centuries owed much of their success to itinerant preachers, and it was clearly true in the Church of Christ in Bedford. Some of these ministers attained national prominence. Within the Church of Christ, Richard M. Gano, who had raised volunteers in Tarrant County and served as a general in the Confederate Army, held several revivals at Bedford and became a national leader among the conservative faction in the church. Local congregations and other church reports indicate that he baptized more than four thousand people, including several in Bedford. Carroll Kendrick preached in Texas, 1850s–1870s, and published the first Church of Christ religious journal in the state. In 1886 in the New Hope Church he directed a ten-day meeting — involving long stretches of preaching, Bible-reading, prayers, baptisms, and singing — which brought in ninety new members. The conservative views held by these men were in opposition to missionary societies and the use of instrumental music during worship services. The *Fort Worth Gazette* reported twice in July 1892, that protracted meetings at the Bedford Christian Church had produced a large number of accessions.

Over three miles to the east, the Euless community never blossomed like Bedford, but continued to attract settlers. In 1881, Elisha Adam and Julia Euless purchased a tract of land south of Bear Creek and built a new home and a cotton gin in the area of present Main and Euless Junior High School. After his settlement there, the community thrived. Local farmers decided to honor the popular young man whose arrival and whose gin seemed to coincide with the end of the hard times. They named their community for him. There was a good water well at the gin that was available to all. A few businesses, such as the T. A. Fuller Blacksmith Shop, clustered around the gin. Cyrus Snow opened a grocery store on the present site of the First United Methodist Church, 106 North Main, and he became first postmaster in 1886. Mail came from Eagle Ford at Dallas and was delivered by horse and buggy to Grapevine, Minter's Chapel, Sowers, Estelle, and Euless. John Evans took over the store and postmastership, 1892–1901.

Adam Euless continued farming until he was again lured into politics. In 1892 he defeated three contenders in a landslide election for county sheriff, and was reelected in 1894. The contests were in the Democratic primaries; except for the brief Populist threat in the 1890s, the general elections of the time were overwhelmingly dominated by the Democratic party. Euless moved to Fort Worth when he was elected and was the first sheriff to occupy an office in the newly constructed county courthouse. Euless never killed anyone in the line of duty, but once he shot and wounded a culprit. After two terms, health problems persuaded Euless to retire from law enforcement and politics. Shortly afterwards, a stroke left him paralyzed and forced him to sell his farm and gin. The gin soon closed. In 1911 a second stroke claimed his life, and he was buried in Fort Worth's Oakwood Cemetery.

In 1884 John Huffman moved from Bedford County, Tennessee, to a farm in an area where the First United Methodist Church of Euless now stands. In 1891 he donated the land in the present 100 block of North Main to the church, across the road from the hall that they had shared with the Presbyterians, now the site of a Mobil gas station. A one-room frame building was erected. Years later Huffman recalled the hour and a half long "hell fire and damnation sermons" and shouting converts. The revivals drew huge crowds in a nearby brush arbor. Members of the congregation were tried in church for moral offenses and were expected to openly repent.

Joe Whitener, who had emigrated from Tennessee in 1881, was a trustee of the Euless School (the old community hall) in 1897, when he persuaded his old friend John W. Calhoun to assume the job of schoolmaster for $50 a month, twice his Tennessee teacher's salary. The Euless School had fifty students in 1896 and either forty or seventy-one in 1897, depending on which list one accepts. A new one-room, frame schoolhouse was constructed on the present southeast corner of Main and Highway 10. Calhoun taught for two years, handling grammar and algebra among other subjects, while also sweeping the floors, making the fires, and maintaining the building and equipment. His students' ages ranged from six to nineteen.

Estill, as noted above, was now misspelled Estelle. Supposedly Amos Burgoon sent in the post office application in an ornate penmanship and it was misread and never corrected. The community post office was revived and considered to be in Tarrant County, 1881–1882, then was transferred to Dallas County until being discontinued in 1904. The Estelle Methodist Church operated from 1870 to about 1915, when it disbanded. The small Estelle Masonic Lodge was established in 1884, located on the present east runway of the airport, in Dallas County. The lodge occupied the second floor of its frame structure and opened a public school on the ground floor (possibly a new site for the Bear Creek School). The Masons paid the teacher for two years until a school district was created. The lodge remained for decades in its rustic setting, then moved southwest in 1958 to downtown Euless, where most of its members lived, and built a brick building on North Main. It had to move again (in Euless) in 1966 because of Airport Freeway construction.

The Bear Creek School continued to offer classes, claiming thirty-one students in 1881 and twenty-six in 1897. The Bear Creek Colored School was somewhere in the vicinity; an early 1900s photograph shows one teacher and forty-six students. In 1886 the Bear Creek Baptist Church was one of twelve congregations founding the Tarrant County Baptist Association. The board attempted to raise $200 to employ a missionary, $10 of which was pledged by Bear Creek. The group drew up a constitution and rules of decorum, one of which was that speakers should "strictly adhere to the subject." But by 1887 several founding members of the Bear Creek Baptist Church were dead and many of the congregation lived on the black prairie a few miles to the east. The church relocated some three miles to the east, in Dallas County. It eventually became the Western Heights Missionary Baptist Church and had to move again (in Irving) in the 1960s because of airport construction.

Five and a half miles southwest of Euless, as the crow flies, the Arwine-Red Sulphur Springs area continued to add farmers and ranchers in the late nineteenth century, but did not become a town. Its schools, like the others around the turn of the century, taught the traditional three "R's" and history and geography, but Arwine's school seem to have been memorable for a certain rowdiness. Lula Hurst Doyle remembered that at Arwine, where the kids ate lunch in the cemetery, they would gang up and pull a young post oak sapling to the ground. One pupil would mount it and the others would send him flying through the air. Many of the flying participants were slow in returning to class after lunch. "Pop the whip" often sent a number of kids sprawling into cactus patches. The school had fifty-four pupils in 1896 and forty-four in 1897.

The Isham Chapel School evidently ceased offering classes in 1891 or 1892, shortly after the Thomas or "Wouldya Have Thought It" School was founded on the southeast corner of the intersection of present Highway 10 and Precinct Line Road, where the Bell Warehouse is today. The nickname arose because of local amazement that the immediate community had two schools. The Thomas School counted about forty-five students in the fall of 1896 and fifty-three in 1897. The school district continued to be called Isham until 1911, and sometimes the Thomas School was not only called Wouldya Have Thought It, but also Isham. To the north the Florence District was created in the 1890s on present Grapevine Highway near Harwood, with seventy students in the autumns of 1896 and 1897.

South of the HEB area, in Mosier Valley, the African Americans maintained themselves almost as an extended family, bringing in a neighboring settler's crops if he were too ill to work or taking food to families in need. On their relatively small farms they grew some cotton and corn as cash crops, but also kept extensive vegetable gardens and the usual farm animals. Many worked elsewhere as well, such as Andy Nelson (c. 1860s–1959), who worked on the "Brown" farm and on county roads, Lottie Nelson for Dr. Rhodes in Tarrant, and Claude Shelton and Richard Johnson for various HEB area farms as well as the Rock Island Railroad. A few, such as John Calhoun Parker and his family, enjoyed true prosperity, by the farm standards of the day. They accumulated over 300 acres, raising a great variety of crops, and built a syrup mill pulled by mules. It

was the only such mill in the vicinity, so farmers hauled cane in from all the surrounding communities. They paid with part of the syrup.

An elementary school was opened in 1883, when Pete Fields gave the Pleasant Springs School an acre on the north side of Mosier Valley Road, a third of a mile west of the later school site. Bell Miller remembered attending the log cabin school in the 1880s, where she learned to read, but not to write, because she was left-handed and the teacher would not let her write with her left hand. Forty-nine children enrolled in 1897, though the school had only fifteen double desks. After district lines were drawn in 1884, Mosier Valley was thereafter included in one of the HEB districts. In reaction to the integrationist impulses of Reconstruction, Texas and the other southern states began passing Jim Crow laws in the 1890s, but total segregation was not yet entrenched. Mosier Valley was allowed to elect a "colored" school trustee to sit on the board during this era. The Mosier Valley School was part of the Bedford district for most of that time, and the Florence and Isham districts maintained small "colored" schools.

Also just south of present Hurst, on the Trinity, Robert Randol took sole possession of the three-story Wheeler's Mill, formerly Leonard's Mill, in the 1870s. Randol's Mill became a popular picnic site and several people settled in the area. For a time a cotton gin operated off the water wheel power. Randol was the community's sole postmaster, 1888–1901. Randol's brother, his brother-in-law, and a number of mill workers died in accidents in the mill. The site gained a scary reputation also because of other untimely deaths, such as the hanging of two horse thieves on a nearby oak.

A study of scattered statistics from nearly all the public schools in the HEB area, 1888–1901, reveals that teachers' salaries varied wildly, apparently based on qualifications, sex, race, and perhaps enrollments, among other distinctions. Characteristics of the individual teachers are largely unknown, but in those instances in which the monthly wages can be calculated, the white male teachers averaged about $50 a month while blacks and women made a little over $40. In this pre-income tax age when men's suits could be purchased for $8, ladies' knit skirts for $1.50, and children's and ladies' shoes for $1.50, something like $40 a month would qualify as a living wage, assuming no need for extended hospitalization or desire for long trips. Of course, the instructor would have to find something else to do for the other eight months of the year when school was not in session. Many accepted fees to tutor students during the other months.

Fort Worth matured and continued growing in the 1880s and 1890s and offered activities that lured country folks into town on weekends. The thirty Fort Worth Fencibles, for instance, drilled on the courthouse square during late summer afternoons and always attracted an appreciative crowd. Sunday afternoon streetcar rides were popular beginning in 1889. Waltzing lessons were taught at Godwin's Hall over a livery stable on Throckmorton Street. Men frequented the White Elephant Saloon, complete with a pit for cock fights, or took in boxing matches or Panthers baseball games. Crowds flocked to various theaters, such as the Fort Worth Opera House, which offered a wide range of material, and the Majestic Theater, which presented vaudeville acts. At the Crystal Springs Emporium the Crystal Springs Ramblers supplied dance music. A buggy ride to Dallas' Blue Room, presided over by Red Calhoun and his orchestra, was another activity which lured country folks into town.

Picnics provided less expensive fun for all. During the summers, boys liked to swim in the area creeks, while girls might be found sewing or perhaps reciting poetry at a literary meeting. Hunting small game was another popular pastime.

On some Saturdays, market days, area farmers undoubtedly drove into Bedford to market relatively small amounts of produce, such as eggs, butter, honey, and vegetables. Those in present Hurst usually drove to Fort Worth or Birdville, while Euless farmers gravitated toward Dallas or Grapevine. When it was time to sell cotton, cattle, or the bulk of the grain, vegetable or melon crops, farmers would usually proceed to the nearest country town with a railroad station, a stockyard, or a grain elevator. Fort Worth was the customary destination in the late nineteenth century. Farmers also rode to town to seek out the male sanctuaries of the era: livery stables, saloons, blacksmith's shops, and barbershops, where they would take their business and gossip on Saturdays.

In the nostalgic memories of many who recollected those years, life was lived out in the subdued light of tree-shaded roads on tranquil afternoons, to the solid clip-clop of horses, the drone of bees and cicadas, the clink of ice in lemonade pitchers, the creak of the porch swings — a time of pause and occasional prosperity. It was an age when gossip was a primary form of amusement and news, a time when food was carried to those families who were caught up in birth, death, or illness.

Despite the bucolic simplicities of rural life in that era, it had its drudgeries and tragedies. Daily experiences on the farm tended to be repetitive and were not alleviated by modern communication, transportation, or entertainment facilities. Running a farm was a difficult, sunup-to-sundown enterprise for most family members. Even the children were expected to hoe, weed, gather corn, pick cotton, and tend to the chickens, hogs, and cows. The family invariably made their own hominy, cooked their own soap, churned their own butter, and sewed their own quilts, beds, and clothes. And, of course, there were the woman's responsibilities of washing, ironing, cooking, canning, and mending as well as the man's job of plowing, planting, harvesting, and marketing of crops. The men also repaired implements and buildings and helped neighbors harvest their crops.

While Drs. Rhodes, Zachery, and Dobkins were often seen dashing around the countryside, making house calls on the sick, their powers were extremely limited. Probably by the twentieth century Dr. William Dobkins had given up applying "mad stones" (stony concretions taken from the stomach of a grazing animal) to wounds to draw off poisons, but the standard treatments of the day weren't much better — castor oil, calomel, quinine, kerosene compounds, mustard plasters, and opium dissolved in alcohol. The average life span in 1900 was around forty-five years. It was not unusual for family members to be swept away by pneumonia, influenza, or tuberculosis.

Still, the Americans in Bedford, Euless, and the Bear Creek, Arwine, Isham, Mosier Valley and Randol Mill communities who witnessed the birth of the twentieth century lived in closely-knit, unified environments. These villagers had not yet experienced cars, highways, radios, utilities, chain stores, and big government. Nevertheless, growing up in the villages instilled confidence and feelings of security in them. That confidence held them in good stead in a world that was changing faster than they knew.

The Good Years, 1900–1920

At the dawn of the twentieth century, in 1901, the Dallas-Fort Worth Interurban line was constructed. Comprised of railway cars electrically powered through overhead wires, it was built south of the Trinity, connecting Fort Worth and Dallas through Arlington and Grand Prairie. U.S. Highway 80 was also completed, parallel to the Interurban. The two new arteries diverted traffic away from Bedford Road, which had previously carried much of the load. Though Bedford Road was upgraded from sand to gravel around 1905, Bedford declined in large part because of the diversion of the traffic. Moreover, the Rock Island Railroad reached Fort Worth from Oklahoma in 1893, then expanded through Texas in several directions. One branch was built along the Trinity River to Dallas in 1903, swinging through the Arwine/Red Sulphur Springs community and near Euless, but bypassing Bedford. By 1909 there appears to have been only one store and fifty residents left around the Bedford business district, and the post office was discontinued and transferred to Arlington at the end of that year.

As the historian T. L. Smith wrote, "By 1900 important towns were aligned along principal railways like beads on a string." Hustling cities like Dallas and Fort Worth owed much of their postwar growth to the railroads. Without a rail line at Bedford, area farmers were compelled to haul the bulk of their crops to the nearest depots; merchants naturally tended to congregate at those same sites. Also, without the traffic generated by a major highway, merchants soon went out of business. The disappearance of towns had been occurring since colonial times and was hardly unusual, even in growing areas.

Bobo's general store and the well beside it did continue serving the remnants of the community, and it remained a rest stop on Bedford Road, which was now primarily just part of the Grapevine-Fort Worth Road. A postman from Fort Worth dropped off mail there every Saturday. Joel Bobo owned the store, 1896–1910, then William R. Fitch, Bedford's last postmaster and W. W. Bobo's son-in-law, took it over, 1910–1933. The well, complete with rope, bucket, and a round wooden lid, was open to the public. Many residents of the area brought their water kegs, which were wooden with iron rings binding them, and hauled off water in their wagons for home usage.

A photograph of the Bedford School's class of 1905 features ninety-seven students and two teachers. In 1912 Bedford replaced the frame schoolhouse with a new two-story brick building at present Bedford Road and Municipal. The new building was erected by Grapevine contractors — Jefferson Estill's progeny, Charles and Frank Estill — for $5,000, and represented the first use of brick in the community. Reputedly each row of bricks was laid just a fraction of an inch inward from the row beneath it, so that each wall angled slightly inward. If so, it is not detectable with the naked eye. This lost art supposedly prevented some settling and cracking. Lit by oil burning lamps, the building featured five classrooms, pine floors, and an auditorium. There was a bell on top and a pitcher-pump well out front. A 1917 photograph reveals thirty-two pupils.

As yet, not much effort was made to fund the schools. Just after World War I, for the three school years 1918–1921, the Bedford school district was expected to contribute a total of about $866 each year by levying taxes of fifty cents for each adult. The state contributed a little over an average of $1,240 those years. The school district was far larger than the hamlet of Bedford.

The churches also left little evidence of their existence. The "Christian Churches" or "Churches of Christ" had been interchangeable terms until a nationwide schism in 1906. New Hope Church opted for the latter, more conservative faction. Distinctions among sects were not always important to lay persons. May Arwine Hackney recalled that there was a Baptist Church in Bedford and a Methodist Church in Hurst, "so we went to one or the other most of the time. If the Baptists had a revival, we would all go to that, and the same with the Isham Methodist Church."

Despite the near demise of Bedford, the area had generated enough population and community spirit to spawn an annual Old Settlers Reunion, beginning around 1912. The meetings were held at the Bedford Cemetery. Strolling through the grounds and reminiscing about those interred was part of the occasion, but so were such activities as baseball games, fiddling contests, picnics, and singing. Water was hauled in barrels from Bobo's well and most people drank from the same dipper. Hundreds would participate, but attendance gradually declined as elderly community members died and younger ones moved away. The last reunion was held during the 1950s.

Bedford was so small that coyotes, wolves, and foxes were still detected but there were enough children in the area to maintain the school and keep things lively. The boys had a baseball club and would go into Euless on Saturdays to play. The pranks of that bygone rural era, such as overturning outhouses at night, are obviously different from today's. Gladys Moore Cannon recalled a brush arbor Methodist revival one Sunday night when two teenaged boys began secretly transferring small children left in the wagons asleep into the wagons of others. Many families arrived home and discovered their own children were missing! The whole area, she said, was in an uproar. One of the culprits hid out overnight at the Bedford School.

Meanwhile, in the county line village of Euless, at the eastern end of a course following present Bedford Road, Murphy Drive, and Huffman (roughly), there was more orientation toward Dallas than in other Tarrant County communities. Groups of farmers would trek to Dallas to buy supplies, sell a few bales of cotton and other crops, and evidently, beginning in the summer of 1910, gather the mail. They traveled together since it required several men to push and pull loaded wagons across the streams. Or some of them, such as John Whitener, Jim Fuller, or Walter McCormick, might go in for a few days just to sell butter, eggs, tomatoes, okra, canteloupes, and watermelons in the Dallas farmers' market, where the products fetched the best prices in the area.

Thomas W. Fuller took over the eighteen-by-twenty foot grocery store and postmastership from John Evans in 1901. It was now in the northwest quadrant of the present Euless Main and Euless Boulevard crossroads. Fuller remained as postmaster until July 1910, when the office was discontinued and moved to Arlington, but for a time Fuller and others were allowed to pick up the village's mail in Dallas and carry it back. The letters were still inserted in the mail pigeon holes in the postal section of the grocery store until rural free delivery was initiated out of Arlington.

Just after Ed Cromer married Sally Fuller in a horse and buggy ceremony, the height of fashion in 1901, he was employed by the Lone Star Gas Company to haul freight. In 1910 the Petrolia gas fields had already been linked to Fort Worth, and the company added a major new market by laying steel pipe to Dallas. It was a high-pressure transmission line destined to last over seventy years. It was necessary to have a trail running alongside to build and maintain the line, and it was called Pipeline Road. Cromer was the first to "walk the pipeline," checking for leaks by listening. Customers purchased gas by placing a quarter in their gas meters. Whenever residents in the area gave directions, the pipeline was a prominent landmark.

In 1903 the Rock Island Railroad built a depot two and a half miles south of Euless at Candon, a hamlet that was platted at that time. The coal-burning engines traversed the Whitener and Will Reaves farms south of Pipeline. The rails gave farmers another option for the marketing of their crops and tended to promote diversification, since the railroad could haul perishables. There was a shift or acceleration away from ranching and perhaps even from cotton farming to diversified operations, fruit farms, and dairies.

In Euless Ed Cromer raised a bit of everything on his 500 acres scattered in several plots in various parts of the community. He was called "Mr. Peach" because of the fine quality of his fruit, which was sold to buyers from all the surrounding counties. A. N. Cannon established a 100-acre nursery and fruit farm in 1900 on South Main, perhaps anticipating the railroad; his rose bushes were shipped all over the southwest and given away for local funerals and weddings. His one-and-a-half story farmhouse at 614 South Main linked Euless with its agricultural past until it was torn down in the 1980s. The retail economy also quickened a bit early in the century when Fuller's grocery store became a general store, Dr. John Scott opened an adjacent drug store, and an ice house and a new blacksmith's shop were established near Fuller's. Tradition holds that Euless had twenty-five people in 1915, but there were certainly more in the community as a whole.

Rock Island opened its line between Fort Worth and Dallas, December 1, 1903, and Candon had its own railroad agent. Ross Duckworth's artesian well, beneath a big wooden tower and metal funnel, provided water for the train. For several years the community seemed to have been a regular stop for most of the half dozen or so daily trains. Candon's name soon changed to Tarrant, perhaps because its mail was confused with Camden's and Canton's. Tarrant had its own post office, 1905–1923, with James Rhodes and his son, Dr. Luther Rhodes, serving as postmasters for over fourteen years. The town's main building, owned by James Rhodes, housed a grocery store, the post office, and a drug store crammed with the usual chill tonics and nostrums. Dr.

Rhodes' office was in back of the drugstore. The Woodmen of the World erected a two-story building, and another grocery store or two operated for years. Tarrant's population, on the north side of the tracks, probably reached almost 100 around 1908, and it also had more businesses than Euless for a time. The twenty-five-foot lots were so small that people had to buy two or three of them to build a house. Grocery store owner Henry Ferris was so enamored with the train that he named his son "Rock Island Ferris," dubbed Roxy by his friends.

But railroad depots did not insure growth. The vicinity's cattle, produce, and passengers were insufficient to justify continued regular service, and by 1911 the trains did not stop unless the agent signaled them. Tarrant gradually began to merge with Euless.

Few church and school records have survived from the era. The First United Methodist Church of Euless continued holding revivals, built their first parsonage in 1915, and erected a new church in 1918. The Candon Baptist Church began with twelve charter members in the home of Charles Fitch in March 1904. A building was completed in 1906 south and east of present day Pipeline Road and South Main and it was rechristened as Tarrant Baptist Church in 1908. Around 1913 the church purchased land on North Main, moved its small frame building with mules and log rollers, and officially became the First Baptist Church of Euless. The Baptists too held zealous revivals, while baptisms were performed in creeks and ponds and Calloway Lake, south of Tarrant.

Sometime around 1908 a school with two teachers was established in the Tarrant community. By 1913 all the Euless area schools south of Minter had consolidated into one district, and a new two-story brick building for whites was built at the present location of South Euless Elementary School, 605 South Main. It offered up to ten grades. There were four classrooms on the first floor and an auditorium and two classrooms on the second floor. The two restrooms were still outside, at either end of the building. A 1917 photograph shows fifty-nine students. For the three school years, 1918–1921, the average property valuation for the district was two and a half times that of Bedford's. The tax rate was fifty cents, and the citizens were supposed to contribute an average of $2,091 to the schools each year, while the state contributed $2,378. There were 218 students in 1920–1921. The Euless, Arwine, and Thomas

districts (the latter two succeeded by Hurst) benefited from taxes on the Rock Island and on sand and gravel excavators.

Some entrepreneurs, such as Dan Harston of Dallas and his brother Bob in Euless, with their horse-and-mule-powered draglines, were among the pioneer excavators along the Trinity. Connecting Euless with the Arwine area was the unnamed, winding, two-lane dirt road that led westward along present Huffman, south on Industrial, west-southwest on South Pipeline, which went straight through (along present Bluebonnet Drive) to Brown Trail, then south on Norwood. The current 900 block of Bluebonnet, which now dead-ends in Rickel Park, often presented a challenge to teamsters and early autos during its heyday as the eastern entryway into Hurst, 1890s-1920s. That stretch of road across Sulphur Branch and up the ridge was called the Devil's Backbone. These roads were graveled in the 1910s.

The Arwine vicinity, like Euless, continued to attract farmers, several small ranchers, and a few sand and gravel operators in the early years of the century. William Hurst's family moved again in the late 1890s to a one-story house just south of the present Bellaire Shopping Center in Hurst and remained there until 1920. His wife Mary helped support the family by selling butter and eggs. "Uncle Billy" turned away from farming toward successful trading and speculating in land and horses throughout the present HEB area. As historian Michael Patterson notes, "The single act for which Billy Hurst is most remembered came just after the turn of the century, around 1903." He and his son Mahlon owned a long strip of land roughly along present Highway 10 at the time that the Rock Island Railroad was laying the line from Fort Worth to Dallas. The railroad company approached Uncle Billy about laying the tracks across his land. He agreed to give the company a right-of-way across his farm, and the Rock Island Railroad agreed to establish a stop there, build a depot, and name it for Hurst. Long time settler Bertha Hendrick believed he was feuding with Jeff Souder and was afraid that Souder would donate land to the east of Hurst's and have the station named after Souder.

The traditional beliefs that Hurst took its permanent name in 1903 and had no official post office in that era are incorrect. The Rock Island at first labeled the site Hurst, but there was already a Hurst 100 miles south in Coryell County that had a post office. The Tarrant County community was soon named Ormel and Jack Loughridge was its sole postmaster from September 1904 until January 1909. By that time the Coryell County hamlet had lost its postal station, and the name of the post office at present Harmon Road and Highway 10, after some discussion in the community, was changed to Hurst. Four months later, in May 1909, the Hurst post office was discontinued and absorbed by Fort Worth.

E. H. Welch was the first railroad agent and operator in 1903. In 1909 three trains ran through Hurst daily from Fort Worth and three more from Dallas, but two of the six stopped only if a passenger was leaving for, or returning from, a five-hundred mile journey to Colorado and beyond or the Missouri River and beyond. Only the night train from Fort Worth stopped without being signaled. By 1911 two trains ran daily from Fort Worth to Dallas and two from Dallas to Fort Worth, with restrictions similar to those of 1909. None stopped regularly, according to extant time-tables.

The railroad depot, with a spacious waiting area, living quarters, and a storeroom, was established at the southwest corner of the railroad tracks and present Harmon Drive, which extended to the tracks at that time. Jack Loughridge, Grady Walker, and a number of others served as stationmasters and telegraphers for the next thirty years or so after 1903. They had various assistants, who worked day and night shifts. Walker and his family lived in the depot in the 1910s, as did others at different times, including a lady telegrapher, Miss Mayes. Three section houses were built on the other side of the tracks east of the station. It was exciting for the community and watching trains come and go was part of the entertainment of the day. Some rambunctious children, such as Gladys Hardisty, hitched short rides on the slow-moving freight cars.

Various cattle pens and warehouses were established on the site, and, of course, were utilized for a time by Hurst-Bedford area farmers and ranchers as the nearest railhead for bulk marketing. Billy Hurst was one of those who dabbled in cattle. According to Homer Hurst, Billy would journey to West Texas, buy cattle from rustlers, and ship three or four cattle car loads to the Hurst pens, where they would be fed, branded, dipped, and partially tamed in a few days. Billy and others who ran cattle, including Ed Hurst, Cliff Peters, Frank Booth, and Marsh Calloway, would turn the

cattle lose in the Trinity bottoms and eventually sell them to Swift and Armour meatpackers in Fort Worth.

Diversified small farms characterized Hurst as they did Euless in the first three decades of the century. Grains, fruits, vegetables, and farm animals were the norm. Among the more prosperous farmers of the 1910s were Mahlon Hurst and his son Ed, who bought a fifteen-ton Rumley steam engine in 1916 to thresh with. They harvested wheat, oats, and barley for the area. But the disappearance of regularly scheduled trains prevented the extensive growth of commercial agriculture other than cotton. Cotton was so durable that it was not dependent on immediate transportation. Hurst area farmers often hauled their cotton down present Precinct Line Road to Randol Mill Road (it was all Randol Mill Road at that time), then southeast up a steep incline for horses out of the Trinity Valley, to the gin in Arlington.

As in the case of Bedford, Hurst was served primarily by one enterprise — Tom Dickey's country store with staple groceries, clothing, farm tools, and a candy jar for the kids. He bought the first car in the village, a Model T Ford, and also established the first filling station in Hurst. Dickey walked with a limp and was remembered for his numerous fishing excursions to Walker Creek and for "helping a lot of people who needed help," as Dub Hurst phrased it. His original store was near the railroad about a half mile from the school. After the post office closed, mail sacks were tossed off the trains and left at the store, which served as an informal substation. Another early business was Jack Loughridge's blacksmith shop.

Hurst's population within its business district was probably no more than twenty in the 1910s, but there were perhaps another 150 to 200 people who considered themselves as living in the Hurst farming community. People in West Hurst still had ties to Birdville and some patronized John Bewley's grocery there and Will Bewley's blacksmith shop.

"Uncle Billy" Hurst was undoubtedly the best known entertainer in the HEB area. He played the fiddle by ear, left-handed and rocking back and forth, specializing in the popular tunes of the day, such as "Turkey in the Straw." Others in the community who played stringed instruments often played with him. He was expected to play on his birthdays, which, during the last decade of his life, became neighborhood events. His family sponsored large picnics. Political candidates gave speeches and newspaper photographs covered the affair. The African Americans of Mosier Valley were invited and usually did the cooking. Open commingling of the two races among adults was a rare event in the South at that time, but Billy and many others in the area seemed to have a more expansive view of segregation than most southern whites.

The birthday party of 1918 was the most memorable. "The Great War" still raged in Europe and Billy used the picnic to raise money for the Red Cross. Some 350 people attended and raised $100. In 1922 the Bedford School trustees asked Billy to play his fiddle at a picnic to benefit the school's basketball team. He said he would be there — at the arbor of the New Hope Church of Christ — if they had to bring him in a coffin. He died in his sleep the night before the affair. After the funeral at Hurst Baptist Church, the picnic stopped while he was buried in Bedford Cemetery, away from all the "Yankees" in Hurst and Arwine Cemetery. A large number of blacks from Mosier Valley were on hand to pay their last respects.

Public school recollections center on the lively times and the consolidations. The Florence School was moved in 1903 to the northwest corner of Precinct Line Road and Harwood, where the junior college is today. The students were remembered for throwing objects in the classroom, tripping teachers with hidden wires, and dancing wildly around the outhouse. One old-timer recalled that the Florence teachers "whipped the hell out of you." There was always only one teacher, who usually lasted only one term. In 1914 declining enrollment and constant problems in retaining instructors persuaded the Florence trustees to disband their district. The students went into the Bedford district on the east and Smithfield and Bransford on the north.

At Arwine School the class picture, c. 1900, reveals fifty-one students and the teacher, Miss Ella Youngblood. During the very early years of the century, Maude Hurst Walker later recalled, there were no grades or report cards. Arwine's teacher promoted students when she thought they were ready. One teacher tended to doze at lunch, which meant that recess lasted two or three hours. The students packed their lunches and drank creek water. There were no bathrooms — the girls went behind the bushes on one side of the school, the boys on the other.

In 1911 or 1912 the Arwine and Thomas schools were abandoned, and a new two-story wooden school was erected equidistant from the two on the current northwest quadrant of Norwood and State Highway 10, where the United Auto Workers hall is today. Each floor had a coal-burning stove. There was an auditorium and one classroom upstairs and two classrooms downstairs. The well was on the schoolground corner and students hauled water in buckets to a push-button drinking fountain with a ten or twenty gallon tank on top. In later years Homer Hurst, Sylvia Souder Emmons, Ruby Sexton Himes, and Hattie Bell Cribbs remembered the Biblical verses recited in "chapel" during assemblies upstairs. The consolidated district and its one school were named Hurst.

The Isham's Chapel Methodist Church sponsored numerous revivals, starting on the first Sunday in August each year and stretching for a week or so. The church's annual homecoming was organized in 1916 by Pastor George Davis and the Ladies' Missionary Society by Mrs. Davis in 1919. Ladies' Aid, as it was called, made quilts and bonnets and aprons, sponsored church dinners, and gathered eggs to help the church meet its operating expenses of a few hundred dollars.

In 1908 the Bedford Baptist Church moved to Ormel, after Elbert Souder and Tom Hurst helped make a deal for some land there. For a total cost of $100, the building was dismantled, moved by wagon, and rebuilt where it still stands in the present 100 block of West Hurst Boulevard. Probably this was a more central location for most of its members, who numbered forty in 1909 and seventy-two by 1919. From 1910 to 1923, however, pastors were intermittent.

Two and one half miles to the east, in Mosier Valley, the Oak Grove Baptist Church and the Mosier Valley Masonic Lodge #103, both of which had apparently been sharing the school building, purchased an acre of land in 1898 and attempted to raise money to build a church–school and a hall. They were forced to build one two-story building around 1900, with the masons meeting upstairs on Saturday nights, the Baptists downstairs on Wednesday and Sunday evenings, and pupils downstairs on weekdays. Fifty-six children signed up for the four-month term in the fall of 1900.

Blacks lost their representative on the Euless School Board in 1904, since the Terrell Election Law effectively ended the right to vote for African Americans in Texas. Ed Cromer, who hired many field hands from the Valley and had his family cook midday meals for them, was a school trustee in 1918 and reputedly took it on himself to replace the leaking shack that served as a school. He hauled lumber in his wagon from Arlington and, with others, erected a new frame building. Around 1900 the Oak Grove Baptist congregation changed its name to the St. John Missionary Baptist Church, then erected its own building in 1911, on the same site that the church occupies today.

Randol's Mill operated until 1920 and Bob Randol died in 1922. The mill then stood vacant until 1934, when it burned. For decades an eighteen-foot shaft of iron jutted out of the riverbed and the rusty turbine wheel remained imbedded there, but neither is visible in the channel today from the Precinct Line Road bridge.

All of northeast Tarrant County was still thoroughly rural, but even at the turn of the century transportation was beginning to mark the land. William B. Cheek, for instance, blazed a road across northern Bedford and Little Bear Creek in the 1890s, officially witnessed by Harvey Sparger. Originally Duke Parker's homestead was known as one of the beauty spots of the county, described by the *Fort Worth Star Telegram* as furnishing "a picture that cannot be duplicated with the artist's brush." But the Bedford Road was opened along the north side of his property around the 1890s and the Rock Island Railroad built its line through the south side in 1903.

Rural residents were required to maintain roads for the county. In 1904 Thomas Fuller and E. A. Euless were responsible for sections of the road between Bedford and the Dallas County line, while Elbert Souder took a portion of the Arlington-Bedford Road. The first autos traversed the area about this time. With their loud gongs and their headlights, they startled some of the villagers. Autos also destroyed the early, unpaved roads. By 1920 the *Grapevine Sun* warned that since cars were now in general use, their owners rather than adjacent farmers should pay for road upkeep. A Farm Demonstration Truck Tour rambled through the area, displaying thirty different kinds of trucks that farmers could buy.

Travel was still precarious in the early twentieth century. Trucks and cars, along with buggies and wagons, could negotiate the unpaved roads in dry weather, through the clouds of dust, but in heavy rains the roads were often impassable. Indeed, before reservoirs were completed west of Fort Worth in the 1930s, the Trinity was untamed — the drought of 1899 was so severe that one could walk on the riverbed, while the cloudburst of September 1913, caused the river to rise sixteen feet in one and one-half hours.

One facet of life that hadn't changed much over the years was the celebration of Christmas, already the primary American holiday. Mary Hardisty in Hurst and Walter Huffman in Euless recalled that early in the century there were no decorations to buy. Wrappings from tobacco or cheese might be utilized or paper chains or strings of popcorn and cranberries. Trees and Christmas parties were offered by the Sunday schools and churches. And there were rounds of Christmas parties at different houses, including such diversions as "spin the bottle" and "candy breaking." There was also square dancing, usually without music, since there were not many musicians in the communities. Gifts often included fruit, mittens, a doll, jacks, china dishes, a vase, a little red wagon, a miniature wagon, and marbles.

There were also youth programs in this era, but gender relations were more constrained than today. The churches held box suppers, which gave the young ladies opportunities to display their culinary talents. The suppers were auctioned and a young man might have to pay dearly to outbid his friends for the privilege of eating with his girlfriend. Young men who were courting learned that they could abandon the horse's reins on their buggies or the steering wheels on their autos and devote all their attention to their sweethearts; the ruts in the roads were so deep that neither type of vehicle, even though moving along, would stray from the road. It was unseemly for pregnant women to appear in public, except when they could work in the fields. If she was determined to get out, her husband might lace up her corset so tight that nobody could detect her condition.

By the twentieth century some families had telephones. Dona Souder Cannon, born in a log cabin where the Hurst Lumber Company is now, recalled that everyone bought their own box units, erected their own poles, and strung their own lines. On their Bedford dairy farm she and A. E. Cannon (named for his father's friend, Adam Euless) had two phones for a time. One was a community phone, while the other reached Birdville and Fort Worth. There were no phone bills. Mrs. Smedley maintained the telephone exchange in Hurst, on the southeast corner of the current Norwood — Highway 10 intersection, and would answer the switchboard any time of night. A 1912 list of Hurst telephone subscribers, reveals fifty-three names. In Euless the J. E. Fuller family bought their first phone in 1912. They also maintained the switchboard in their home, and people would ring them to connect their line with another party.

HEB was so shielded from world events that when old-timers are asked the traditional question of oral histories — what was the effect of World War I on your lives? — about all they can note was the temporary shortage of flour and sugar.

The brief school "years" were also out of touch with the evolving world and ill served the communities, but harvesting the crops partially with child labor was still considered more important than education. The fading railway and postal services illustrated the area's lack of growth, but HEB avoided the fate of many communities, such as Randol Mill, Tarrant, and Estelle, that lost their identities when left behind by railroads and post offices. The tranquil horse and buggy age had ended, and the villagers were soon to learn that they no longer resided in a haven unaffected by the anxieties of economic and social change.

c. 1908. First Baptist Church of Hurst's roots run deep, as did the faith of its early members. Sometime before 1890 nine people organized the Pleasant Run Baptist Church in an old log cabin near Bransford. They united with other small community congregations and built a church in Bedford sometime between 1884 and 1889. This picture may have been taken in Bedford. The members moved to Ormel (Hurst) in 1908 to the present 100 block of West Hurst Boulevard, then moved again in 1936 to make way for the construction of Highway 183. The church remained at present Highway 10 and Holder Drive for fifty-three years, then moved to the fast-growing northern sector of town, near Norwood Drive and Harwood Road in 1989. Part of the congregation remained in the older complex and established Hurst Baptist Church. The First Baptist Church of Hurst believes that God has given it a special task to be a Bible-teaching, Bible-preaching, and God-worshipping church. — Courtesy First Baptist Church of Hurst

1895. The Sam Street Company's map of Tarrant County in 1895 depicts the Bedford community as a cluster of farms and small acreages, with the heart of the community along a strip of Bedford Road spanning from the Bedford School on the west to the New Hope Church of Christ on the east, each symbolized by small circles with crosses – or bell towers – on top. Home owners were marked by rectangular symbols, renters by triangles. – Courtesy Tarrant County Junior College

1890. Bedford College, which opened in 1882, was generally a college preparatory institution, heavily emphasizing Greek, Latin, and philosophy. The building mysteriously burned in 1893 following the dismissal of an instructor, and the Bedford Public School was built in its place. This 1890 newspaper photograph is the only known photograph that pictures the two-story building. – Courtesy Tarrant County Junior College

ca. 1897. Bedford School students all looked ready to go, as bright as their newly painted shiplap schoolhouse, when this photograph was made in the late 1890s. Who can explain why the school's windows are boarded up?

– Courtesy Tarrant County Junior College

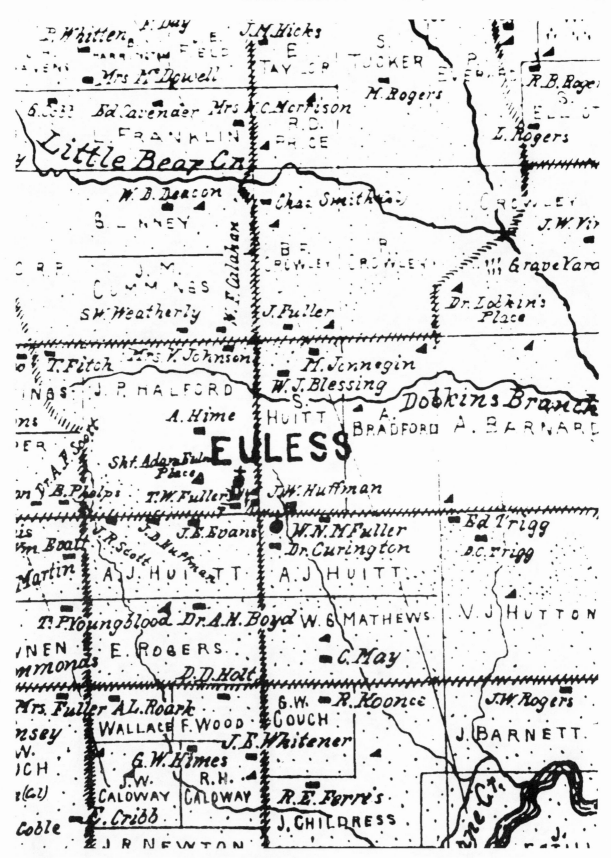

1895. Sam Street Company's 1895 Tarrant County map shows a few homes and businesses clustered around the Euless Methodist Church and Sheriff Euless's gin. The graveyard in the upper right is Bear Creek Cemetery.

— *Courtesy Tarrant County Junior College*

1880s. In 1881 Elisha Adam Euless (1848–1911), who hailed from Bedford County, Tennessee, bought a tract of land in Tarrant County south of Bear Creek, engaged in farming, and built a cotton gin just north of the site of present-day Euless City Hall. – Courtesy Weldon Green Cannon Collection, Tarrant County Junior College

1910s. Using separate photographs from the period, Jack Bryant of the Hurst Friends of the Library painted William L. Hurst (right) and Grady Walker standing in front of the Hurst Station. The community was eventually named for Mr. Hurst. – Courtesy Jack Bryant, Hurst Friends of Library

ca. 1894. Elisha Adam Euless was the first county sheriff to use the present Tarrant County Courthouse, completed in 1894. Here he poses (fifth standing from left) with his deputies, son Marvin (second from right), and the jail's cook.

— Courtesy Tarrant County Historical Commission

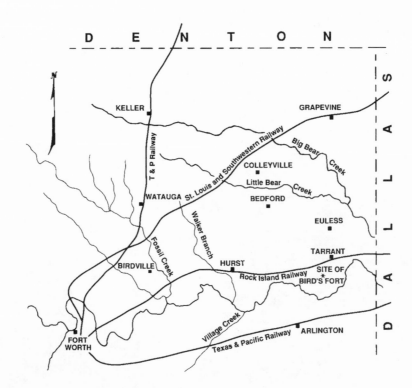

ca. 1905. With the construction of the Rock Island Railroad line between Fort Worth and Dallas in 1903, a total of four railroad systems traversed Northeast Tarrant County. While Bedford and Euless languished in part as a result of being bypassed by the railroads, Hurst owes its identity to the Rock Island's creation of Hurst station.

— Courtesy Tarrant County Junior College

1895. Sam Street Company's 1895 Tarrant County map indicates that much of the area now known as Hurst was at that time identified as Randol; several wagon roads converged at the mill. Only "Hurst" Lake on the nearby J. A. Hust survey used the Hurst name, and Hurst in this case was a corruption of Hust. Fed by an artesian spring, Hust Lake was the site of a sportsman's clubhouse. Arwine School is located in the upper right. — Courtesy Tarrant County Junior College

Above: 1979. Preservationists in Bedford long sought to honor the heritage of the old Bedford well that had been dug beside Bobo's general store. A new stone cover and a bronze plaque dedicated to its history was placed over the well in 1979.
                                                                    – Courtesy Duane Gage

Below: 1912: Bedford School built in 1912. School board members met with building contractors upon completion of Bedford School construction. The structure served as a school until 1969, when it became a service center for the city. Much of the heart and soul of the community was bound up in the Bedford School. – Courtesy Michael E. Patterson

1910. Over three dozen old-time settlers from HEB, particularly from Euless and Tarrant, are shown in this extended family photograph. Dr. Luther Rhodes (with mustache) and his wife Margaret (Calloway?) are seated to the left, with son Leslie in her mother's lap and Lorena in front of her father. The four girls in front, from the left, are Callie (Fuller) Whitener, Jennie (Fuller) Webb, Jessie (Jernigan) Eden, and Daisy (Fuller) Poland. On the second row from the left are the Fuller boys – Homer, Warren, Clifford, Bascomb, Jesse, Bobby, Cecil, Horace, and Raymond. On the third row from the left are Bill Fuller, Thelma (Fuller) Webb, Ruth (Fuller) Millican, J. R. Fuller, Virginia (Fuller) Payton in lap, Fay (Jernigan) Eden, Grandpa Moody Fuller with wrap for abscess or jaw cancer, Grandma Sarah Fuller, Tom Fuller, Mary Alma Fuller, Amp Fuller, Ida Jernigan, Bettie (Fuller) Jernigan with baby Ross in lap. On the fourth row are Arthur Fuller, Sulia Fuller, Ross Fuller, Marion Jernigan, Jessie (Fuller) Terrell, Mary (Fuller) Jernigan, Essie (Fuller) Weatherly, Evie (Fuller) Sweaney, Mamie (Jernigan) Alexander, Effie Fuller, Myrtle (Fuller) Hanson, Osie (Lindsay) Fuller, Hubert Fuller, and Roy Fuller. Some of the ladies' married names were acquired later in life. — Courtesy Troy Fuller

1910. Shortly after the Rock Island Railroad built a line south of Euless in 1903, the station there was named Tarrant, and the company hoped that Tarrant would become the most active thriving commercial center in the county. The commercial growth never materialized, however, and Tarrant Depot closed in the 1930s. Grady Walker, shown here, was stationmaster at both the Tarrant and Hurst depots at different times.

— Courtesy Weldon Cannon Collection, Tarrant County Junior College

ca. 1913. When several one- and two-room schools consolidated to form the Euless Public School District, the newly consolidated district could boast of an impressive two-story brick building with six classrooms and an auditorium. From 1913 to 1934 it offered up to ten grades. From 1934 to 1957 it was the only high school in HEB. The picture was taken for a post card. – Courtesy Mary Ruth Ellis Collection, Tarrant County Junior College

ca. 1905. To escape the stress of Reconstruction, Tennessee ex-Confederate William Letchworth Hurst (1833–1922) came to Tarrant County in 1870, bringing his wife, Mary Ann Lynch Hurst (1835–1908) and their seven children in a covered wagon. The family located first in present Euless, then Bedford, before acquiring farm land near the Trinity River. There Hurst raised corn and cotton and speculated in land while his wife handled the butter and eggs and child rearing. The community was eventually named Hurst in 1909, six years after the Rock Island Railroad built a line across some of Hurst's property. — Courtesy Tarrant County Junior College

ca. 1905. Jeff and Mary Souder migrated from Indiana around 1880 and took up farming in present Hurst. Among their adult living descendants today are Bill and Roger Souder, Maxine Souder Jennings, Ellen French Paul, Leonard French, Lynn Cannon, Ruby Cannon Summerour, Margie Cannon Wooley, Jo Ellen Emmons Greer, Ruby Sexton Himes, Ellsworth Jones, and Jimmy Wilkerson.
— Courtesy Evelyn Fitch-George

ca. 1920. Flossie Dickey Longley's painting of her father Tom Dickey's country store in Hurst reflects the nostalgic era of her childhood, the morning mist of a new day dawning, horses tied to the hitching post, and jalopies raising dust on the country road. — Courtesy Flossie Longley

ca. 1904. When public-spirited Daniel Arwine arrived from Indiana in 1865 and settled on a homestead near the present intersection of Brown Trail and Pipeline Road in present Hurst, he donated six acres of land for a school, church, and cemetery. The Arwine School, also called the Sulphur Springs School, was the first public school in the area. Arwine typified early civic-minded pioneers who felt responsible for providing such basic institutions that comprise a civilized community.

— Courtesy Tarrant County Junior College

ca. 1910. Leonard's Mill, built by Archibald Leonard in 1856, allegedly was burned in 1860 by slaves who had been stirred up by Yankee abolitionists. The mill was rebuilt and operated for over fifty years as a bustling commercial enterprise. Industrious mill hand R. A. Randol purchased the mill in 1872, built a blacksmith shop on one side of it and a cotton gin on the other, and operated it until 1920. Citizens from miles around had flour and corn meal ground for them at Randol's Mill.

— Courtesy Tarrant County Junior College

Top photo: *ca. 1890. The Isham Chapel School, which operated in the early 1890s, apparently did not have a dress code requiring shoes, at least for the elementary children.* — Courtesy Tarrant County Junior College

Middle photo: *ca. 1912. Until about 1915 the one-room Florence School was located on the northwest corner of Harwood Road and Precinct Line Road in Hurst, where children walked to school or rode their donkeys. Today on the same corner Tarrant County Junior College's Northeast Campus carries on the more diversified eduction of the late 20th century.*
— Courtesy Weldon Cannon Collection, Tarrant County Junior College

Bottom photo: *ca. 1915. By the end of the century, no matter where one lived, there seemed to be a one or two-room school within walking distance. When a second school was built in the Arwine community in the 1890s, it was named Thomas School, but old-timers dubbed it "Wouldya Thought It," in wonder that the community had two schools.*
— Courtesy Tarrant County Junior College

III. The Hard Years, 1920s-1940s

Retail trade barely survived in HEB in the 1920s and early 1930s, and farming was far from prosperous. By the early 1920s in the village of Euless one-legged former Deputy Sheriff John "Deb" Cruse had operated T. W. Fuller's old general store for years. A cast-iron wood stove was in the center, and for a time in 1923 the county library opened a branch in one section of the building. Miss Willie Huffman, the librarian, let people check out books twice a week. She earned $6 a month. The store closed soon afterward.

Its niche in the community was soon taken by Homer Fuller in 1926. He had to abandon his 160-acre farm when he was crippled by polio. When he could no longer farm, he had a twelve-by-fourteen foot store built on the southeast corner of the Euless-Grapevine Road (present Main) and Euless Boulevard.

For a time in the 1920s Clark "Red" Franklin's blacksmith's shop was located next to the Methodist Church, but at different times Red had set up shop at Calloway Lake and Birdville. Ray Reed and Wayne Arthur soon opened a little garage, servicing Model "Ts" on a dirt floor, just south of Fuller's grocery.

Most services, including medical, were still scarce in the area. The *Grapevine Sun,* for instance, noted in its occasional "Euless News" column, April 5, 1923, that "an optometrist will be at Board and Austin's (Grapevine) Drug Store Saturday April 7th, one day only this trip."

Meanwhile, many HEB area farmers, like those in the rest of the country, were forced off the land in the 1920s and 1930s, victimized by low crop prices, foreign competition, and declining property values. Walter McCormick and Warren Fuller were two of those who relinquished the agrarian way of life in the 1920s. McCormick, whose family had been in the area since his great grandfather helped found present Colleyville, left Euless and got a job on the Texas and Pacific Railroad. He and his wife Willie Mae did not return until 1948. Fuller tried the Dallas Ford Motor Company's assembly line for three months, then returned to Euless to go into business with his brother Homer.

For those who persevered, farming became an increasingly speculative business enterprise. Many abandoned the raising of fruits and vegetables, which were frequently brought in by trucks from the Rio Grande Valley. Some farmers took up dairying, which grew in the postwar era, since expanding cities consumed more milk and cream, and imports were not a threat.

Shortly after Fuller's grocery opened, the Tennessee Dairy receiving plant was built across the intersection where McDonald's is today. Comer Horton was the dairy's manager. The company's few drivers picked up tepid milk all over the county, cooled it, and hauled it to Dallas. Refrigerating and condensing milk with gasoline engines was difficult, and the company wanted electricity. The dairy farmers could also use electric service for milking and for grinding feed. Fuller also wanted it and the Texas Power and Light Company (TPL) advised him that it would cost $2,500 to bring electricity to Euless. Homer Fuller immediately visited with Tennessee Dairy and most of his neighbors and collected the money within a few hours. TPL service began in Euless in September, 1929, over forty-three years after it began in Fort Worth. Fuller volunteered the use of his store as a place for customers to pay their electric bills.

Homer Fuller, soon joined by his brother Warren, c. 1927, kept Fuller Brothers Grocery and Feed open twelve hours a day, six days a week, and eventually employed four or five hands. It also sold men's working clothes, shoes, socks, gloves, garden tools, and some hardware, dry goods, and patent medicines. Twenty pounds of sugar or dry beans could be purchased for a dollar. One of the Fullers would make three trips weekly in the truck to fetch merchandise, mostly from stores and meatpackers in Fort Worth. They also had cattle and swine slaughtered in Grapevine. Gulf gas pumps were installed in front of the store. The store was the social center of the community, where neighbors visited every evening. On Friday the Fullers would dispatch all their checks by the mailman to the Arlington Bank, since there were no banks in the HEB area. The mailman, implementing rural free delivery beyond the law's requirements, would bring back change the next day. The brothers ran the general store for twenty-nine years, remodeling it three times.

The Great Depression of the 1930s drove crop prices down and further disrupted the area's economy. For instance, a prime dairy cow during this time might bring $16. One farmer, unable to sell or feed his shoats, simply released them in front of Fuller's store. Some twenty-five percent of the county population was on relief. President Franklin Roosevelt's New Deal government began raising farm prices in 1933 by curbing production. Scores of HEB cattle were assigned to the slaughter. The cattle were buried in a twenty-foot ditch near the present intersection of 360 and Airport Freeway. One cow was buried near the surface with a leg sticking up, so that one unemployed man with a wife and three children could secretly and illegally retrieve some meat for his family.

Along South Pipeline Road in Euless, Ed and Sally Cromer seemed to thrive as farmers despite the hard times. It helped that the Cromers owned a considerable amount of good land and had a knack for retailing. They operated a dairy, raised a variety of vegetables, and maintained vast fruit orchards. People from surrounding counties and states hauled their produce back by wagon and truck. Peddlers from Dallas would buy peaches for peach brandy. The Cromers supplied Safeway's Dallas stores. Cromer was the village Republican and was angered by the efforts of the Demo-cratic Roosevelt administration to raise farm prices by cutting production. Cromer was one of three men from the Euless area assigned to slaughter a certain number of cattle from each herd in 1933, but could not accept the task and resigned from the group.

Euless nurseryman Ross Cannon was another who successfully defied the Depression. As he put it, "During the early thirties I got an itch to see the Chicago World's Fair. Money was short as frog's hair. But rose bushes and shrubs were plentiful." He persuaded American Airlines founder C. R. Smith to swap tickets to Chicago and elsewhere for plantings on his bare office grounds.

Still other farmers survived by brewing whiskey in homemade stills and selling it locally. During Prohibition, 1919–1933, the nation was legally dry, but there were millions of Americans willing to buy bootleg alcoholic beverages. On one occasion prohibition agents caught a Euless farmer with twenty barrels of mash that was ready to brew. They split the barrels open. Hogs got into the mash, however, and the combined stench traveled a considerable distance, as did the sound of drunken pigs.

Warren Fuller recalled that for a nickle a customer could buy two loaves of Mrs. Baird's bread or a quart or more of milk, but nickles were hard to come by. Dairy hands, for instance, milked cows about eight hours a day, beginning at 2:00 A.M., and received $3 a week. One dairy farmer with 200 cows and five or six hands feared he would go under when another employer offered his boys $3.50 a week.

Dairy farming was stimulated by New Deal programs that promoted farm diversification and purchased "star boarders and scrub stock" from the farms. Federal money was also plowed into Dallas' Texas Centennial project at Fair Park, where exhibits stimulated considerable consumer interest in dairy products in 1936 and 1937. By the end of the decade Tarrant County was the center of the biggest milk and butterfat producing area in Texas.

A number of farmers and farm hands took jobs with such New Deal work relief agencies as the Works Progress Administration. About fifty of them would congregate on weekday mornings at Fullers' store, 1933–1940, where the government trucks would gather them up and haul them to various road building and other construction projects in the county. They received a dollar a day.

With the surveying and paving of present

Highway 10 and the slight easing of the Depression in the middle and late 1930s, other businesses dared to open. Jack Robinson opened a cafe just west of Tennessee Dairy. As one of the two places open at night, it attracted teenagers who sipped cokes and played the nickelodian. Lee Byers launched a burger stand with six stools on the southwest corner of present Main and 10. It is now 101 West Euless Boulevard, the Custom Load Works.

In the next few years the Fuller brothers and Weaver Birch, the Democratic precinct chairman, opened gasoline stations in the same area, and Reece Fitch installed gasoline pumps in front of a small grocery store he opened. Earl Stapleton and Andy and Luther Morelock opened garages. The latter was Ray Reed's former business, moved from the southeast to the northwest quadrant of the intersection. Ben Reaves opened an ice house behind the burger stand, buying his ice in Arlington, and Curtis Greer installed a barbershop in his house, immediately south of Fuller's store. Greer gave the shop up during the war, and shortly thereafter Fred Gray opened a barbershop in the western half of a new building next to Birch's garage. The Hamrick family unveiled the Euless Variety Store in the eastern half, next to the burger stand that Byers turned over to Raymond Fuller in the early 1940s. During the winter of 1944–1945, Fort Worth businessman Dave Hawes, anticipating the construction of Amon Carter Field, erected the Euless Lumber Company where it still stands at 200 West Euless Boulevard.

Slow growth continued during the war, and in the late 1940s the volunteer fire fighters built the station that stands where the old Woodman Hall used to be on Highway 10 near Main, Wilkes Berry opened a cafe just west of the station, vying with Emma's Cafe in Hurst as the best truckstop between Dallas and Fort Worth. Ernest Allman opened a barbecue-apple pie joint west of the lumberyard where the Waffle House now stands. The buildings utilized by Birch, Berry, Hamrick, and Gray were erected by Ross Cannon, who owned most of the southwest quadrant of the main intersection. James Berry maintained a washateria briefly on the east end of the village near present Cullum and 10, while Jess Tillery opened one that operated for years at the west end, next to Allman's Barbecue on present Huffman.

There were no more than 100 people in the village in 1930 and maybe a few more in 1940. After the stimulus of war, there were perhaps 300 people in Euless (counting Tarrant) by the end of the 1940s. One Euless lad, Billy Eden, was killed in action in the war. Weldon Cannon writes, "About 1950 Ross [Cannon] platted the second addition to Euless (I think the first was by Alexander and Huitt in southeast Euless) along South Main, West Euless Boulevard, and Ross Avenue. He built rent houses along South Main and Ross Avenue." Euless was growing in the late 1940s, but unforseen problems were awaiting.

The Euless First Baptist Church built a new structure in 1922, seating 200, but usually the pastors continued to be students at Southwestern Baptist Seminary. Worship services were shared with First United Methodist across the street, with each church providing a preacher every other week. In 1931 a fundamentalist faction under Pastor Bert Kimball, admirers of the fiery Fort Worth Reverend J. Frank Norris, split from First Baptist. The Central Baptist Church was established just north of the Methodist Church. First Baptist's membership was cut in half, but eventually revived, and several building additions were completed in the 1940s. The Methodists organized a women's missionary service in 1927 and built a new parsonage in 1951. Wartime growth prompted the founding of two or three other small Protestant congregations. The churches, along with Fuller's Store, were the social centers of the village.

The Euless School continued operating on South Main, usually through the tenth grade. The board of trustees under T. E. Whitener was determined to achieve high school status. An auditorium was built in 1930. In 1932 power lines were extended south from the business district to the school, an artesian well was dug, and a four-room teacherage was erected to attract and house a new superintendent, his wife, and four teachers. Also launched that year were a Parent-Teacher Association, a glee club, a literary society, and a dramatic club. The school qualified for eleven grades and high school standing in 1934. State law required twelve in 1941, and Euless High School added one grade and continued to be the only high school in present HEB. The school averaged fewer than two and half graduates per year, 1934–1941, but a little over nine from 1942–1950. In 1947 a gym was added.

Holiday parties as well as money-raising carnivals, which evolved from the Drama Club's 1932 Halloween program, were traditional highlights of every school year, along with the clubs' events and performances. The first yearbook and newspaper began in the 1947–1948 year. Superintendent O. B. Powell and eight faculty taught 149 students in 1947–1948 and 181 two years later.

The town of Tarrant faded after the loss of its post office in 1923 and the evacuation of the railroad section hands about a decade later. It was already smaller than Euless by 1930. Mrs. George Jarvis owned the grocery store in the village's main building during the 1920s. Community excitement rose in the mid-1920s when Mrs. Jarvis demanded that two teenagers, Lewis Cribbs and Truman Ward, be thrown in jail for allegedly inserting electric box slugs instead of nickels in the chewing gum machine. The constable determined that they were innocent. Electricity arrived in the village in 1937. It had no more than twenty-five people in 1940.

The biggest employer in the Tarrant area was the Fort Worth Sand and Gravel Company (FWSG), organized about 1922, probably absorbing some of the efforts of earlier independent operators. It excavated the gravel pits along the Trinity bottoms south of Euless and Hurst around the clock. The gravel was sized through screens, washed free of sand, and, for a time, loaded by men with shovels into boxcars at sidings below the Tarrant and Hurst depots. Rock Island freight trains picked them up at night.

A large washing plant, complete with steam Monoghan draglines, was built in 1929 south of Hurst, just east of present Precinct Line Road across Walker Branch. Marsh Calloway — a little man who walked peculiarly since he had fallen from a water tower and broken his back and legs — owned much of the land and sold gravel to the company by the yard. Calloway soon learned to hire a gravel checker to count the five-yard buckets on the Monoghan.

Dan Harston's Trinity Gravel Company, working the old Parker tract south of Hurst, was also a sizeable operation in the 1920s and had its own washing plant in the Trinity bottoms south of Parker Cemetery. Bob Harston of Euless served as foreman for brother Dan's company, then later as foreman for FWSG in charge of building railroad spurs. Homer Hurst recalls that building those railroads was the hardest work he ever performed. East of the FWSG washing plant, just south of the current Bell plant, Central Concrete began a smaller sand and gravel operation in the 1930s, and several other small companies were in the area. Some Euless residents dumped trash in the abandoned excavations, and children swam and rode horses in them. Bonnie and Clyde may have hid out in some of them in the 1930s.

The Hurst economy seemed a bit slower than Euless' in evolving away from truck farming toward dairying. "Huse" and "Em" Hurst inherited lands along present Highway 10, including the site of the current Bell plant, and hauled their melons, corn, and plums to Dallas or occasionally Fort Worth. Elbert Souder cross-bred several varieties of plums and peaches. Reginald Anderson's family owned about 300 acres bounded by what is now Redbud Drive on the north, Highway 10 on the south, Simmons Drive on the east, and a creek west of Precinct Line Road; they invariably carried their produce and milk into Fort Worth to sell.

As in Euless some farmers were not really making their living by farming. Dub Hurst recollected that his uncle's and father's farms were more noted for their stills than their tomatoes. As a youngster Dub earned $10 a night hauling mash in ten-gallon milk cans from the barrels, where it was fermented, to the stills. The illegal whiskey sold for $10 a gallon. Dub remembered, "There was no other work . . . and it was mostly a case of survival because there was not any money in the country at that time." Occasionally a neighbor would turn someone in and a constable would smash his bottles with an ax. One persistent constable was killed by a bootlegger in the Trinity bottoms. Dub believed the biggest problem was that "everyone in the community would steal whiskey from each other." One of his neighbors, a prominent Baptist, confessed years later that he had stolen a five-gallon jug that Uncle Em had hidden in his pea patch. Em had spent hours searching for it, after having swiped it himself. One Riverside man maintained a still to the west of the present Bell plant, on the creek next to the old site of the Baptist Church, and chased off boys such as Bill Souder who wanted to hunt squirrels.

Square dancing, typically accompanied by drinking and carousing, was an entertainment of the era, but it was frowned upon by most white people. Some dances were held in Homer French's store in Hurst. More dances were held in Mosier Valley, where square dancing was held in higher esteem. Each race maintained its own events and its own fiddlers and string bands. Many of the men in the area met in barns or out in the woods or in Mosier Valley and shot dice, played poker, and bet on bulldog and rooster fights. Perhaps the most surprising facet of these contests was that they were integrated, with black males from Mosier Valley participating fully. The churches "saved" some men from these sinful activities and marriages, e.g. Homer Hurst's marriage to Daisy Smith, saved some.

A less benign force also took deadly aim at sin. A wave of fear swept through the U.S. in the 1920s, carried along by a twisted super-Americanism that was violently critical of Catholics, Jews, foreigners, and blacks. Its leading vehicle was the Ku Klux Klan, and in Texas the Klan also sought out bootleggers and gamblers for tar-and-feathers and other punishments. For a time the Klan took over the city governments of Dallas and Fort Worth and was very potent in Texas. The Klan whirled through the HEB area, and tied up and whipped some of Dub Hurst's acquaintances. The movement played out in 1925, but it was a reminder that rural areas were no longer so isolated from the world.

A growing number of settlers evaded farming if they could. T. J. Page moved to Hurst in 1920 and intended to farm, but landed a job with the Fort Worth Post Office. William and Emma Souder as newlyweds in 1920 went to work at the Farmers' Market in Fort Worth and also farmed some. Elijah and Minnie Souder Wilkinson farmed, but "Lige" was also forced to work as an independent plumber during the 1920s and 1930s. Reginald Anderson gave up farming in the 1930s and took a job with the Dallas Post Office. Dub Hurst — among other activities — delivered wagonloads of stove wood to Fort Worth boarding houses for $5 each and sold cottontail rabbits that he had trapped for twenty-five cents each. He tried farming briefly, then went to work for an oil company in Burkburnett in 1927. Kenith Hurst drove produce trucks. J. C. McCurry was an independent carpenter, L. W. Oehlschlaeger ran an auto and furniture upholstery shop, and Cy Rickel owned Big Three Welding, all in Fort Worth. Some residents, such as Homer Hurst and Ray Thomas, who was superintendent of the washing plant, worked for FWSG.

Tom Dickey's grocery and feed store was the heart of the business community along the western end of the still unnamed main road of the 1920s and early 1930s between Hurst and Euless — roughly present Hurst Boulevard, Brown Trail, Bluebonnet-South Pipeline meandering through to Industrial, and Huffman-Euless Boulevard. Dickey's store and filling station was actually on the railroad near the depot until he moved it a half mile northwest in the 1920s, just west of the

Baptist Church, where Trinity Forest Industries is today at 205 West Hurst Boulevard. Dickey prospered to the extent that he bought a new car at Slaughter Motor Company in Arlington, August 25, 1924, for $465.40.

Nearby, Jack Loughridge's blacksmith shop was still in business early in the decade. Adjacent to the school on the southeast, Huse Hurst opened another grocery as well as a filling station with one hand-cranked pump around 1919, but was more interested in his watermelons and dominoes and too generous with credit. He closed his store in the mid-1920s. Dickey retired in the early 1930s. Homer French maintained a grocery-feed-gasoline stop just east of the Baptist Church from the mid-1920s until around 1932. There may have been a lumber company south of the school, by the tracks, for a time in the 1920s or early 1930s. E. E. Cunningham installed another small grocery and filling station at present Bluebonnet and Brown Trail in the late 1920s, then moved it to the northeast corner of present Norwood and Highway 10. He rented the grocery to Pryor Reeves in the late 1930s, while selling lumber in an adjacent building to the north. The retail lumber operation was closed about 1940. Around 1944 Cunningham built a cinder block building for an Army Surplus store. It still stands at 107–111 East Hurst Boulevard, where Clark's Furniture Refinishing and Brazil's Cleaners are today. George Bolton started a grocery-hardware store around the late 1930s at present 141 East Hurst Boulevard, in the building housing Al's Radiator now, and stayed until about 1950. Each grocery owner had to drive into Fort Worth every few days to stock up on goods.

In 1936, with $150, William and Emma Souder opened a grocery store at the present site of Tuggle Automotive, 125 West Hurst Boulevard. They spent $75 on the block building, $50 to stock it with groceries, and kept $25 in cash. The Souder store grew to include a service station by 1939 and an adjoining cafe in 1944, with a total of ten employees. The store was open seven days a week and maintained canned goods, meats, vegetables, and a few hardware items. While Emma managed the business, at first from 6:00 A.M. to 10:00 P.M., William worked as a carpenter on such projects as the building of the new Hurst School. Emma's Cafe featured large ten cent hamburgers with all the trimmings. Emma's was a favorite coffee and lunch stop for Dallas-Fort Worth truckers on present Highway 10, paved in 1939.

At the old Hurst School at present Highway 10 and Norwood most pupils, carrying their books and lunches, would arrive by auto. Hattie Bell (Reeves) Cribbs recalls six or eight of them lived east of the school in the 1920s and were often hauled in by Nuck Sexton in his Model T Ford. It had no brakes, but Nuck used the middle clutch to throw it in reverse and bring the vehicle to a shuddering stop. In the last year of the old school's operation, 1939–1940, nine grades were taught by four teachers. The new brick school, erected by WPA workers in 1940, was on the site of the old building. Still with four teachers it offered grades one through eight. Upon graduation Hurst students — if they received more education — usually went on to Paschal or Birdville High School (now Haltom High) or Fort Worth Riverside. The facility later became South Hurst Elementary School and today is the office of United Auto Worker locals.

The students' swimming hole, about thirty-feet long and ten-feet deep, was dredged in Walker Branch by Marvin and Homer Hurst in the 1920s. At Hust Lake near Randol Mill there was a private club, but also community swimming and fish-fry picnics.

Hurst's library was founded in 1927 as a county station, and books were available by request from the Fort Worth Public Library. When Inza Page Powell became the first librarian, the collection consisted of two wooden boxes with 100 or so books, stashed in the cloakroom of the school and lit by a gas lamp. It was open one afternoon per week and most of the patrons were students, many of whom would come in the summer on horseback and bicycles. Adults visited more in the winter, when farm chores slacked off somewhat. In 1940 it was given a room in the new Hurst School. By 1948 it contained 200 volumes and circulated 800 books per month, mostly westerns and mysteries.

Charles Matthews pastored the Hurst and Birdville Baptist churches, 1921–1923, and toted a gun back and forth for protection against bootleggers. The Hurst congregation gained its first full-time pastor, Reverend Henry Brannon, 1931-1934, and slowly grew to the point that some Sunday School classes were held in vehicles. The church was wired for electricity in 1936 and an auditorium was built during the war, but the church suffered after Brannon left and did not call another full-time pastor until 1947. The building is the abandoned edifice named King-Whaley in the present 100 block of West Hurst Boulevard.

Isham's Chapel Methodist Church used wood stoves and kerosene lamps as late as 1935. One night in 1935 a lamp exploded and set the pulpit on fire. FWSG then allowed the church to tie in on its electric line. Many attended both churches during revivals as well as the Bedford Church of Christ and the Baptist church in Mosier Valley. The latter featured more fervor and shouting than the HEB churches. Just after the war Grady Walker and T. J. Page established the First Church of Christ in Hurst at present Brown Trail and Holder.

Hurst probably had fewer than thirty people in the immediate village in 1930, and perhaps one hundred south of Pipeline a decade later, but there were dozens more than that within the current city limits. The first electric lighting was provided for two houses by T. J. Page's Delco plant, a small building in his back yard, but Texas Electric soon entered Hurst in the early or mid-1930s. There were only two telephones in "town" in 1930, and they were on a party line system for the area. Each family had a certain number of rings, which was a code to tell who the call was for.

Many Hurst boys served in the war, and R. B. Bryant and J. C. McCurry were killed in action. The war stimulated the local economy somewhat. W. C. Norwood built a grocery-cafe-Gulf station attached to Emma's Cafe in 1945, on the site of Homer French's store, the part of the block building where Shelton's Upholstery is today. Mrs. Norwood is remembered for her homemade pies despite her arthritic hands.

Next door a Mr. Oliver launched Hurst's first newspaper in 1946, but his one room was so crowded that some of the machinery was outdoors, creating a junky appearance. After a few months, landlord Charles Norwood ordered Mr. Oliver to put all the machiney outside and the fledgling paper died.

With the 1947 announcement of the impending construction of Amon Carter Field, Lindley and James Lucas sank their savings into building the Hurst Lumber Company, launched with one truck and a small load of lumber. It is the oldest continuing business serving the town (though actually located in Fort Worth), now thriving at 104 East Hurst Boulevard. The airport was not completed for six years, and James Lucas remembers the cold day in 1949 when the company did five cents worth of business.

The Mosier Valley black community traded

in the HEB stores, and helped HEB farmers when called on to slaughter hogs or harvest crops. White males watched Mosier Valley revivals and participated in the gambling games, cock fights, and fox hunts. White families would venture into Mosier Valley on special occasions, such as July 4th, when they would participate in the festivities and consume Shortjack Wallace's barbecue. Black and white children occasionally played with each other, as they did in much of the South. The Reeves farm, for instance, adjoined Mosier Valley, and young Hattie Bell Reeves and her friends played with the Farrow family children, Ikey and Gracie, and others from Mosier Valley in the 1920s. Mosier Valley probably reached its peak population from the mid-1920s to the mid-1930s, with some 300 people.

Education in Mosier Valley was a festering problem. In the 1940s, for instance, Ollie Farrow walked ten miles a day to Haltom City, where he worked for a dollar a day to earn his children's bus fare to the Fort Worth secondary schools. A twenty-five-by-fifty-foot frame structure, probably erected by Ed Cromer and others in 1918, still served as the main part of the Mosier Valley Elementary School. It was ramshackle by 1949, with no heating, lighting, or sanitary facilities. Two teachers struggled with forty-five students through seven grades. Probably as late as the summer of 1949 no one in either Mosier Valley or HEB realized that the two communities that seemed to placidly coexist were on the verge of a bitter break.

From Mosier Valley and Hurst, the sandy road with no name now called Brown Trail meandered north to the Bedford Road, which led northeastward to Bedford. Truck farming still dominated Bedford. A. E. and Dona Souder Cannon's tomatoes, canteloupes, and watermelons, for instance, were often sold to truckers from Kansas and Oklahoma, and Thurman Allen's canteloupe patches employed many young boys in the area.

Dairying was prevalent too. One problem in the industry was the inspection process. State milk inspectors appraised cleanliness and took bacteria counts in random, unannounced visits to dairy farms. If the milk was condemned, the inspectors put a red dye in it to keep it from being sold. Then farmers could not even feed it to farm animals. Usually farmers managed to discover when an inspector was making the local rounds. On one occasion, with the farmer absent, an inspector condemned a Bedford dairy's milk, and when the farmer caught up with him a brawl occurred.

The business district in the community was the present 1900 and 2000 blocks of Bedford Road. William R. Fitch continued running Fitch's General Merchandise and his well. The original building was torn down and replaced in the 1920s. The second building stands, remodeled, at 1937 Bedford Road and houses Dorothy J's and Bowen Structures. William turned it over to his son and daughter-in-law, Walter and Evelyn (Souder), in 1933. Groceries and feed were their mainstays, but a Texaco station became part of the operation in the 1930s. Their butchers handled fresh meat, which was available (thanks to a friend in the Fort Worth slaughterhouses) even during wartime rationing.

The store was the social center of the village. Several community picnics were held there, complete with fiddle music. Elections were held there — voters occasionally marked their ballots on feed sacks — and were also held in the schoolhouse. The store was located at the intersection of two rural postal routes and functioned as an informal substation. During World War II in particular, people brought packages there, where they purchased wrappings and stamps, and the rural carriers would haul them to the Arlington station. The Fitches operated the store until 1963 — it was in the family some ninety years.

Ed M. Bilger, who had been laid off at the Ford assembly plant in Dallas, was driving through the area on the first Sunday in January 1927, seeking a site to open a garage. He happened to stop at Fitch's store and Fitch told him that the building across the street had just become available for rent and that the Bedford area could certainly use a garage. Ed and Dora Bilger opened a filling station and garage January 10th at present 1944 Bedford Road, beginning fifty-one years of old-fashioned full automotive service. The garage, constructed of squirted concrete blocks with holes through the centers, still stands. It was the third full-service station in the northeastern quadrant of the county. Cities Service and later Humble gasoline were sold for decades, beginning with one Armstrong pump with the ten-gallon jar on top and a price of fifteen cents per gallon. Dora Bilger worked alongside her husband in the garage and was a certified mechanic, unusual for a woman at that time. Both had attended a mechanics' night school in Fort Worth. The Bilgers built their house alongside the garage in 1930, for

$1,739. It's the oldest brick home in Bedford. Bilger later served as a town councilman, a volunteer firefighter, and a school board member, and he raised huge lemons as a hobby.

Frank DeCamp had maintained a blacksmith's shop on Bedford Road in the early 1920s and was evidently succeeded by Charles "Bum" Schmidt by the middle of the decade. Schmidt's shop was just east of Fitch's store, on the site of the old fire hall. Schmidt retired by 1930. Just west of Bilger and east of the present fire station was A. J. Griffin's Dew Drop In, a small grocery store and lunch counter. He sold the property and the store closed around 1940.

There were probably no more than eighty residents in Bedford as late as 1940, but the stimulus of war caused the population to advance to about 200 during the decade. Business activity picked up slightly. James Simmons and his brother-in-law Ralph Barr built and opened another grocery store in 1945 at present 2008 Bedford Road. Their wives, Heralee and Oleta, joined them in working there, and the store operated for thirty-three years. Although the community received electricity in 1936, not all area farmers were served, so the store sold them kerosene lamps and blocks of ice to cool their dairy products.

By the late 1940s the Bedford 4-H Club had evolved into a Home Demonstration Club of women and children. Sewing, cooking, preserving food, furniture upholstering, and interior decorating were among its activities. Prize-winning entries were submitted in county baking and sewing contests. When Walter Fitch built a new home, his wife Evelyn, Bernice Hardisty, Irene MacManus, Dora Bilger, and others began a library in 1950 in the old Fitch residence, which was moved next to Fitch's store. The Bedford School offered anywhere from seven to ten grades in this period (usually nine) and became an eighth grade school in 1947. The PTA was organized in 1921. There were usually two or three teachers. Principal Herb Williams and his family made their home in a classroom for a time in the 1920s. The girls wore dresses and the boys usually overalls. Lunches of biscuits and sausages or jelly sandwiches were packed to school. If they received more education, Bedford students, like those from Hurst, went on to area high schools, though no school buses were available until the 1940s.

The Bedford Church of Christ, still officially the New Hope Church, offered its regular services without the lapses that characterized many country congregations. The tabernacle on the side of the building continued to be the center for outdoor worship in warm weather as well as the site of the Old Settlers' Reunions. Community volunteers maintained the cemetery, often working together on a cleaning day. (In 1936 a leading citizen noted that "Bedford's best is in the cemetery.") The Birdville Baptist Church sponsored the First Baptist Church in Bedford in the 1940s, in a building that had been used as a chicken coop. The Oak Grove Methodist Church moved to Colleyville in the 1940s.

During the Depression, but independent of it, a distinct construction technique reached its peak in Northeast Tarrant County. A widespread phenomenon locally, but relatively rare elsewhere, was the use of local sandstone, usually applied as a veneer on wood siding. Within HEB, Hurst was the site of such surviving structures as the Roe house (1933), 601 Caduceus Lane, and Felps house (1942), 401–403 Long Boone Road, veneered by Colleyville stonemason Walter Reynolds.

What leisure time HEB residents could find was passed in community activities. Someone would organize an ice cream supper, barbeque, or perhaps a moonlight picnic or community play almost every Saturday night. "Spin-the-bottle" was a party game, while softball, basketball, volleyball, marbles, jacks, and mumbley-peg prevailed at the schools. Few scores have survived, but in March 1925, Euless beat Bedford twice in basketball, 25–10 and 21–4. Euless High's "A" basketball team posted a 7–26 record, 1947–1950. The girls had basketball teams too; their shorts extended almost to their knees and were one of the few exceptions to the code that required girls to wear dresses. Pranksters were still around. Bedford's "dirty dozen," for instance, took Hugh Souder's buggy apart and reassembled it on top of Fitch's store in the early 1920s. The Four-H clubs encouraged students to enter their products and livestock in the Fort Worth Fat Stock Show each winter. Every October the Texas State Fair in Dallas and the Grapevine Community Fair attracted HEB residents, and between 1933 and 1937 some would slip away to Arlington Downs, during the era that betting was allowed on horse racing.

There were many services, of course, that the villages could not provide. People had to leave town just to get a haircut, often journeying to Clarence "Barber" Cobb's shop in Smithfield. Cobb cut women's hair too, in the era before beauty parlors were available. During the Depression he accepted chickens in exchange for haircuts. One house rule during Cobb's decades on the job, 1920–1985, was that politics and religion could not be discussed.

The Rock Island Railroad, meanwhile, had spread through 8,000 miles in fourteen states by 1920, but it shed its rural passenger stops as it installed streamliners. Four Rock Island engines still thundered through Hurst and Tarrant daily in the 1920s, but the two from Fort Worth made no stops in the county. The 11:00 A.M. train from Dallas would stop in Tarrant if the agent flagged it down with his lantern and in Hurst if one was a paying passenger traveling a considerable distance (defined elaborately). The night train from Dallas would stop at either of the two depots only upon the signal of paying passengers journeying afar. Kenith Hurst worked as a "snipe," scrubbing down the Hurst depot once a week for $2.46. The Hurst and Tarrant depots were abandoned in the 1930s. By 1934 there was only one daily locomotive each leaving Dallas and Fort Worth, and the only stop, pending a signal, was in Irving. Some of the demand was met by Bowen Motor Coaches, which stopped in Hurst and Euless when passengers awaited. Fuller's store sold tickets and flagged the buses in Euless. Fort Worth businessman Temple Bowen also established a pioneer air carrier in 1927, Texas Air Transport, the leading forerunner of American Airlines.

By the early 1930s both Dallas and Fort Worth desired a paved "north road" between them, but the route generated controversy. By 1934 there were three proposed routes. Consulting engineer E. P. Arneson urged the direct and least expensive northern route, a straight shoot from north Dallas through Euless and Bedford to a point on State Highway 121 over two and a half miles northeast of Birdville. Dubbed the Bedford route, or prophetically, the airline boulevard, it was embraced by Bedford leaders, including W. R. Fitch and A. J. Griffin. A contending possibility followed the same course almost two miles past Euless, near Bedford, then dipped southwest to Pipeline Road, north of Hurst at that time, to 121, about one and a half miles northeast of Birdville. Elbert Souder and the Reverend S. P. Brown, who lived on Pipeline, headed this cause, which was also backed by some engineering surveys. The third route moved southwest from Euless to Hurst and thence to Birdville and was supported by T. J. Page, Bob Lucas, and Ed Cromer among others. The decision was foreordained

when Fort Worth leaders concluded that the Bedford route was a Dallas effort to bypass the Fort Worth business district on the north. They demanded the costly Hurst route, and State Highway 15 (renumbered 183 in the early 1940s, now 10) was asphalted and took its present configuration in 1939. County Commissioner Frank Estill was caught in the crossfire, endorsed all three routes at different times, and was defeated for a fourth term in 1938 by fewer than 150 votes.

The major north-south artery, the Arlington-Grapevine Highway (present Industrial) was asphalted by 1937. The metal from the old iron bridge that had spanned the Trinity since 1889 was used to build a new bridge across Little Bear Creek in north Euless, or perhaps the bridge was moved intact. It served North Main Street traffic until the timbers began to deteriorate, and it was moved to South Euless Park in 1975. Much of the construction on these highways and other area roads was funded by the WPA. More spectacular was the replacement of every wooden bridge and culvert in the county with steel and concrete structures. Twelve hundred men worked for eighteen months, 1938–1940, in a project that attracted national attention as a work relief measure and an engineering feat.

The vast government spending of World War II, 1941–1945, introduced full employment to the Dallas-Fort Worth area and renewed farm prosperity. The federal government, for instance, built the Consolidated Aircraft (now Lockheed) bomber plant near Lake Worth in 1941, when America was preparing for war. During the war, several people from HEB worked there and on other nearby defense jobs. Also, various military bases in the area purchased food and supplies from local farmers and businesses. Traffic on old Highway 183 increased considerably. Thus even as it required rationing gasoline, tires, and sugar, the war boosted the local economy, and the HEB population, while still minute, more than doubled during the decade.

Reginald Anderson returned from the Pacific and found that Hurst, destined to be the first of the three villages to expand, was "still rural, but slowly and surely becoming a bedroom community." J. H. Spencer, a bricklaying contractor, saw the possibilities in 1948, built a home for himself, bought property, and began building houses on Hurstview as well as Hurst's first small water system. Sam Harmon built some on Harmon Road and Walter Vinson on Norwood Street. City gas and telephone services were obtained in 1949, and a civic league chaired by J. A. McCalip was formed to promote development. Old Highway 183 was paved with concrete in 1950, leading eastward to the construction site of Greater Fort Worth International Airport, but large scale residential construction was held up by the absence of immediate demand, water and sewage facilities, and FHA loans.

Truck driver Bill Austin moved to Hurst in 1949 to try his hand at managing Emma's Cafe.

His daughter recalled her shock in moving from the city of Fort Worth. Hurst numbered perhaps 250 people. The sudden change seemed like the end of the world to Miss Austin, but that world was about to change again, more dramatically than she or J. H. Spencer could have imagined. Most residents would have agreed with Em Hurst years later when he was asked if he had ever believed the HEB area would one day become heavily populated and commercialized. "Naw," he cracked, "it wasn't even a good cornfield."

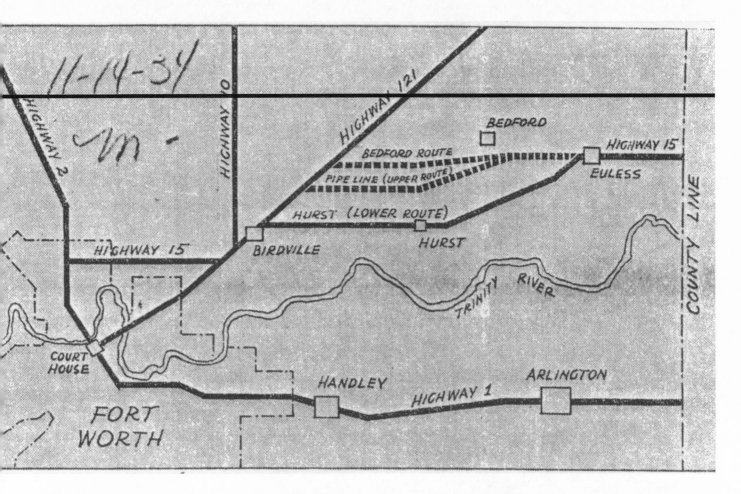

1934. The Hurst or lower route for the location of old Highway 15 between Fort Worth and Dallas, shown on the above map, was formally designated by the State Highway Commission in Austin. Shown by the dotted lines are the other routes proposed during the designation controversy of several years standing. Bedford was bypassed again in 1939, just as it had been over thirty years earlier by the railroad. Hurst and Euless were thereby in better position to develop sooner than Bedford, although in the long run every metroplex location between the two major cities was destined to grow prodigiously.
– Courtesy *Fort Worth Star-Telegram* Collection, Special Collections Division,
University of Texas at Arlington Libraries

ca. 1945. Leon McGinnis bought the Humble Station, grocery, and attached home in the rear from Reece Fitch around 1945 and remained in downtown Euless four or five years. The Woodman of the World building is in the background to the right. — Courtesy Homer L. McGinnis and the Euless Historical Preservation Committee

ca. 1945. The Euless Lumber Company, since remodeled, is the oldest continuously operated business in Euless. Bill Byers is the veteran operator and owner. — Courtesy B. L. Byers and the Euless Historical Preservation Committee

late 1930s. Homer Fuller stands in front of his grocery store in the heart of Euless during late Depression days. — Courtesy Mazie Eden and the Euless Historical Preservation Committee

ca. 1920s. In Euless Ed Cromer's diversified farming operations centered around his Pipeline Road homestead, called Ten Oaks, for the large post oaks that anchored his fences around his house and outbuildings. The barnyard abutted the road, as indicated by the mailboxes set at the barnyard fence. – Courtesy Tarrant County Junior College

1947. Several buildings were unroofed, a house moved off its foundation, and this building, Andy and Luther Morelock's garage, was virtually demolished by the twister that hit Euless in mid-April, 1947. — Courtesy *Fort Worth Star-Telegram* Photograph Collection, Special Collections Division, University of Texas at Arlington Libraries

ca. 1942. Looking northeast in downtown Euless, one sees the Tennessee Dairies, Luther and Andy Morelock's garage, and the First Methodist Church. — Courtesy Boyce Byers and the Euless Historical Preservation Committee

1936. The Euless School basketball team featured back row from the left, Red Lewellen, Billy Eden, Tub Huffman, J. N. Pierce, Leon McGinnis, and J. T. Simmons, and front row from the left, Bovel Fuller, Leon Whitener, Johnny Nobles, and R. E. Uselton. The coach was Lee Witt.

— Courtesy Jean Whitener and the Euless Historical Preservation Committee

ca. 1930s. Using real horse power on his farm operation, Guy Reeves would accomodate a spring colt with a lunch break while the nursing mare remained harnessed for a full day's work.

— Courtesy Mary Ruth Ellis Collection, Tarrant County Junior College

ca. 1920. The James M. Anderson family, seen here in front of their two-story box house in Hurst, participated in the transition of the community from pioneer times into the twentieth century. Many Anderson descendants are among today's area population. The family farm consisted of about 300 acres and included a sizeable portion of present South Hurst.

— Courtesy Tarrant County Junior College

ca. 1920. Tom Dickey's farm truck, seen here filled with sweet potatoes for the Fort Worth market, signified the advent of northeast Tarrant County's future reliance on motorized vehicles. — Courtesy Tarrant County Junior College

ca. 1940s. William and Emma Souder (parents of Hurst mayor Bill Souder) opened a small grocery store across the road from Hurst School in1936, and it soon became a focal point for the community. Emma, seen here with a grocery salesman, managed the store and always had a friendly smile for customers although her work day often began at 6:00 A.M. and lasted to 10:00 P.M. closing. — Courtesy Tarrant County Junior College

1922. The starters for Hurst School's 1922 girls basketball team are dressed in appropriate attire – modest, cumbersome suits and white "tennis" shoes. In girls basketball at that time forwards, centers, and guards were restricted to limited zones on the court, since it was considered unladylike and too taxing for young women to run all the way from baskets at each end of the court. — Courtesy Tarrant County Junior College

1939. One of the more successful local teams, the 1939 Hurst School boys basketball team, won a double round robin tournament undefeated and represented their school in the Fort Worth area district finals. Tall players were rare on small school teams. The bench warmer on the right end of the back row is Hurst's present mayor, Bill Souder.

— Courtesy Tarrant County Junior College

ca. 1920. Since Reconstruction days the Oak Grove Baptist congregation in Mosier Valley served the black community in spiritual and humanitarian affairs. It changed its name to St. John's Missionary Baptist Church around 1900, and in 1911 this structure was built, with tall arched windows pointing to heaven. — Courtesy Tarrant County Junior College

1937. The charter members of the Hurst Home Demonstration Club included, on front row left to right, Mrs. Harris, Mrs. Harris' mother, Mary Hardisty, the child Mary Ruth Reeves, Bertha Reeves, Maude Booth, and Adeline Morris. Second row from left to right includes Georgia Stevens, Johnnie Bacon, Mattie Norwood, Mrs. B. H. Watson, Willie Reeves, Mrs. Atkins, Alice French, Mrs. Jack Davis, and Mrs. Halton Dominy. Back row from left to right includes Mrs. Leroy Smith, Mabel Morris, Belle Souder, Essie French, and Annie Souder--all "first ladies" of Hurst. They enjoyed sewing demonstrations, book reviews, card parties, and programs on ways to use household appliances, now that electricity had come to the community.

— Courtesy Mary Ruth Ellis Collection, Tarrant County Junior College

ca. 1940. Fitch's grocery and feed store is depicted here, as seen from Ed Bilger's home. The service station was on the left, obscured by the tree; the gasoline pump on the right was no longer in use, nor was the old icebox. On the far right is a water pump house that tapped into the old Bedford well.

— Courtesy Mr. and Mrs. Ed Bilger and
Mr. and Mrs. Ed Bilger, Jr.

1930s. Elbert and Annie Souder's farm, which included peach and plum orchards, was located near Arwine Cemetery, and they donated the land for the road to the cemetery. The tub was used to water the stock.

— Courtesy Evelyn Fitch-George

ca. 1920s. Upon the merger of the Isham District (Thomas School) and the Arwine District (often dubbed Red Sulphur Springs School) the original Hearst School was erected, complete with belfry.

— Courtesy Hattie Bell Cribbs

ca. 1929. Ed Bilger, Jr., stands beside his father's Cities Service pump at the family station and garage in the old heart of Bedford. The family's first home is in the background. The garage still stands, but the pump and extended roof are long gone. Ed Bilger, Jr., later served as a Fort Worth policeman for thirty years, a Bedford volunteer fire fighter, and most recently as Bedford's Fire Chief.

— Courtesy Mr. and Mrs. Ed Bilger and
Mr. and Mrs. Ed Bilger, Jr.

1927. Bedford School students, on the front row from the left, Truman Ward, Mary Jane Acton, Ruby Cannon, Vera Caudle, Bessie Hackney, and Evelyn Wilkerson. On the middle row, unknown girl, Clifford Roy, Goldie Hackney, Bernice Caudle, Ted Vanhorn, and Walter Fitch. On the top row, Lynn Cannon, Ben Acton, unknown boy, Dawson White, Lillie Bailey, unknown girl, Vada Caudle, and Aurelia Bailey. White was principal and teacher, and Lynn Cannon recalls that he often taught sitting down with his feet propped up on the desk. Bedford School contained nine grades in 1927, but not everyone in the picture is a ninth grader. — Courtesy Evelyn Fitch-George

1949. Bedford's Home Demonstration Club met in various homes and at different times of the year. At this gathering shortly before Christmas, on the back row from the left, Mrs. Kirk, two unknown ladies, Helen Garrett, Jerry McMillan, Oleta Bilger, and Oleta Barr. On the front row, Neva Jean Howard and son Dane, Frankie Fay Wills and daughter, Evelyn Fitch and son Walter, Hattie Bell Cribbs and daughter Lennie, Jackie Hinds and son, and the veternarian's wife and her son. In the forefront is Helen Garrett's daughter. — Courtesy Evelyn Fitch-George

ca. 1915. Rural farm life in the late 1800s and early 1900s was a dawn-to-dusk enterprise, and every member of the family old enough to perform a chore pitched in. Hattie Arwine Anderson (1868–1960) prepared for spring plowing by sharpening plowshares. The Anderson farm was located in western Hurst, where today the major traffic intersection of Interstate 820 and Airport Freeway propels tens of thousands of metroplex residents on their busy way.

— Courtesy Tarrant County Junior College

ca. 1940. When the Hurst School was built by the WPA 1938–1940, for $35,000, it was the pride of the community. Within thirty years several new elementary schools were built around its attendance zone and Hurst Elementary closed due to declining enrollment. It was a special education center, 1969–1975. The 1940 structure was purchased by the United Auto Workers in 1977 for use as their union hall. — Courtesy Tarrant County Junior College

1941. Picture Day at Bedford School in 1941 found Edna Anderson's 6th, 7th and 8th graders dressed in appropriate attire – print dresses for the girls and bib overalls for the boys. – Courtesy Tarrant County Junior College

ca. 1950. Self-help was a common theme for the women's groups of Mosier Valley. This bake sale was conducted as a fund-raiser for a deserving community project. — Courtesy Tarrant County Junior College

IV. Years of Boom and Tumult, 1950s–1960s

"Take a good look at Hurst. It will never be the Hurst as you have known it." Those were the words of Principal C. C. Bodine of the Hurst School in March 1951, after reading to his students the announcement in the *Fort Worth Star-Telegram* that Bell Aircraft Corporation would build a helicopter factory valued at over $3,000,000 in the community.

Incorporation appeared necessary to prevent Fort Worth from annexing Hurst as well as to clear the legal path for enfranchising a water supply company. Not everyone was in favor of incorporation. Several people owned tin buildings that they were afraid would be condemned and some did not want to start paying taxes, but at the school building on May 4, 1951, Hurst voters approved incorporation 36 to 24. T. J. Page became the first mayor.

Clearly the helicopter plant (at 600 East Hurst Boulevard) and Amon Carter Field (at the eastern end of present Highway 10 in Euless), both of which opened in 1953, hastened the inevitable boom. So did the proximity to Fort Worth and the concreting of present Highway 10 (then Highway 183) and Farm-to-Market Road 157. "The fifties and sixties were focused on population," according to one newspaper. "The builders and developers had almost a carte blanche in shaping Hurst." And supposedly the helicopters had trouble getting into the air because of the soaring land values. Many old-timers sold their land or businesses for a hefty profit and moved into new homes. Some tried to escape the changing times by moving farther out, away from the rapidly approaching "city slickers and yankees."

In October 1951, Jess Holder announced plans for the erection of Hurst's first shopping center, a $500,000 finishing touch to his development of 210 lots across from the Bell plant (then fifty-five acres). In November, with a water system about to be installed, the Kenyon-Cockrell Development Company, veteran home builders with offices in Hurst, announced that two houses would be built in December as "guinea pigs" for a fifty-two-unit Hurst View Addition. It was a great success, and by February 1952, the company started cutting into Eastwood Hills, a 150-acre tract of wooded land. Individual entrepreneurs, such as Bell employees John Barfield and Herman Smith, also eased into the real estate business. By late 1953 half a dozen residential additions were under development for homes ranging in price from $7,000 to $30,000. One reason the town grew was because housing prices were 25 percent cheaper than in Fort Worth and because the city actively sought FHA and GI Bill mortgages in the area.

Businesses began to locate near old Highway 183 in Hurst and Euless. The post office was revived in 1949, with Bill Souder as postmaster. The Hurst Chamber of Commerce, organized with twelve charter members in the fall of 1952, encouraged the growth and was soon accompanied by a new Euless Chamber. In the spring of 1952 the Boyles Galvanizing Company built a $150,000 commercial hot dip galvanizing plant on a tract between old 183 and the Rock Island tracks. The Stirling Motel was founded on old 183 just east of 157 and, in a few years, the grand Astoria Hotel and Restaurant was established across the street from the Bell plant. Brad Harston started his own sand and gravel business in and around Hurst, 1952, and pioneered the restoration of land as a company policy. W. O. Ferguson's Red-D-Go Concrete, 1953, and at least two other sand and gravel companies began about the same time in the Hurst-Euless area. So did such companies as Henry Metals, Anchor Metals, Horton Brothers Milk Transport, and Tri-Tronics Laboratories as well as a couple of Phillips and Sinclair oil operations.

Among Hurst retailers Bolton's store was succeeded by the Belhurst Cafe for a time in the early 1950s, then Curtis Brown's Hurst Pharmacy, c. 1954, the first drug store in town. When Brown moved to Pipeline, Harry Edwards launched Hurst Radio and TV in 1955. Al's Radiator Service is in the same building today at 141 East Hurst Boulevard. Edwards still runs Hurst TV, now at 101 West Pipeline. In 1951 Harry Yates opened his drive-in grocery, which is still in business at 151 East Hurst Boulevard. L. E. Brazil and his son Bob founded the town's first cleaners in 1954, and Bob operates Brazil's Cleaners today in the old Cunningham building at 111 East Hurst Boulevard, the oldest business in Hurst under one owner. Lone Star Gas secured the Hurst franchise in 1952. Jake Brewer established the company's first "office" in 1955, a desk in Bob George's Grocery Store, where he picked up orders each day to work on appliances or install meters. The grocery was located in the Souders' building, where Tuggle Automotive Machinery Service is today.

In 1955 the Hurst and Euless Chambers of Commerce merged. An early brochure noted the importance of nearby industries, such as Menasco Manufacturing Company, which made aircraft parts, the General Motors assembly plant in Arlington, and Texas Industries, which had purchased Fort Worth Sand and Gravel in 1953. Hurst-Euless, the brochure observed, was in the center of a two billion dollar retail market that was not plagued by income or sales taxes. It also noted that unions were kept in their place by such features as the right-to-work law, prohibition of mass picketing, and prohibition of the checkoff without company consent. The 1956 Hurst-Euless map and business directory listed forty-eight enterprises.

Hurst's first tax bills were mailed in October 1951 — $1 for every $100 valuation — to help pay for the water system and fire fighting equipment. The Volunteer Fire Department assembled in May 1952, collected $17 to buy equipment, and elected Postmaster Bill Souder as fire chief. The men were eager, but not knowledgeable, so $200 in fire damage might be followed by double that

in water damage. Citizens voted for the first bond issue, 87 to 0, for $250,000 for a new high school in 1953. Usually, though, if the town needed something in those days, the quickest way to get it was through old-fashioned barbecues and parties.

One day in late May 1954, Hurst stores closed for a civic groundbreaking ceremony. Volunteers supplied much of the labor and materials for the concrete-block city office building finished the next year on Holder Drive one block north of old 183. It was the first of several such complexes constructed in the next three decades. Joe Watson was the first full-time city employee and constituted the entire Police Department in 1953–1954.

The 2,000 aircraft employees who went to work for Bell in 1953 were soon organized by the United Automobile Workers. The UAW quickly became active in community affairs. In 1955 it took the lead in planning a recreation and youth center for Hurst. By the time the Teen Canteen was launched in January 1958, its dances and games were also supported by the city park board, the Chamber of Commerce, and many churches and civic clubs.

Yet commercial development did not materialize as fast as expected. Hurst was essentially a "bedroom community," mostly south of Bedford-Euless Road until the late 1950s, where "You could fire a cannon down a busy thoroughfare at midday and not hit a soul." It was estimated in 1958 that of the 8,500 people who lived in Hurst, 40 percent worked in Fort Worth, 50 percent in Dallas, and 10 percent in Hurst. Much shopping had to be performed in neighboring towns. Water supply was a crucial problem, but by the end of the decade new industries and commercial developments were creating job opportunities within the city, and the numbers were sufficient to attract large supermarkets.

Meanwhile, in December 1956 the city abandoned its 1952 general law charter (designed for small towns that were not growing) and received a home rule charter, authorized by a vote of 215 to 164. Before the election, a Hurst city official announced that the charter was not being changed to annex land. The report was termed a "pure rumor" spread by people opposed to the charter change. The change created a permanent city manager post, increased city council membership from five to seven, and allowed expansionist-minded city fathers to annex by ordinance without permission of land owners. City councilman Jere Green and others were already known to be upset about the recently established narrow strip of Fort Worth city limits that blocked Hurst's southern expansion, but Fort Worth would not yield its link to the renamed airport, Greater Southwest Field. (In its expansion Fort Worth annexed Mosier Valley and Tarrant, despite their historic ties to HEB). The only possible substantial geographic growth was due north, and the town immediately began annexing land north of Bedford-Euless Road and, indeed, taking land all the way up to the western reaches of Grapevine. Southlake hastily incorporated in September 1956, to stave off Hurst. Grapevine, Southlake, and Colleyville were all general law cities and could not annex without permission of land owners, but in 1957 they were petitioned daily by area residents who preferred one of the three municipalities. Some of the petitioners' lands had been annexed by Hurst. At a turbulent February 1957 meeting of nearly one hundred officials from thirteen towns, convened to work out difficulties, Hurst Mayor W. E. Vincent, a real estate developer, blamed Fort Worth for beginning the encroachments. Then the mayor added, "That's right, another greedy city to the west of us acted first, and . . ." Laughter drowned out his words, but the tenseness returned when Vincent stood fast on Hurst's annexations. The representatives of twelve towns stormed out of Hurst's First Baptist Church, denouncing the town's officials. By 1958 Hurst reversed its untenable policy and deannexed areas, e.g. Smithfield, in which residents requested reincorporation or incorporation with another municipality.

The established churches boomed along with the surge in population. First Baptist, during the span of Don Houser's pastorate, 1953–1957, moved to the current site of Hurst Baptist at Holder Drive and present State Highway 10, more than doubling its membership. Isham Chapel moved within the city limits in 1952 and became the First Methodist Church. During its first decade, membership soared from 160 to 900, even though fifty members broke off and launched St. Paul's Methodist Church. Continued growth forced First Methodist to move again in 1964 to its current location at 530 Elm Street.

Suburbanization spawned some dubious activities. In 1955 Hurst police (both of them) prevented a gang fight by arresting three teenagers in possession of blackjacks and tire chains. That same year the annexation of land along Mason Lane somehow led to the bizarre installation of a long line of utility poles right down the middle of the street. In 1957 Hurst and Euless police closed a cafe on old Highway 183 that was also operating as a bawdy house. In 1965 Internal Revenue Service agents with sledge hammers splintered the door of a luxury apartment house in Hurst and exposed a gambling den and two bookies.

Land purchases began in 1958 for the tract on Mary, south of Pipeline, that became Central Park. A civic center was completed at 700 Mary Drive in 1960 and housed all city offices except the police department. The library was taken over by the city at that time. For awhile it had only one study table and was partitioned from dance classes and other programs by chicken wire. By 1960 the city had adopted a master plan for a twenty-five-year development of streets, drainage, parks, and municipal offices. A bond issue to finance the first five years passed in 1960 by a four-to-one margin, despite the fact that it would definitely raise taxes, and still another issue was floated in 1962. A new city hall was built on Precinct Line Road in 1966.

By 1960 the population topped 10,500. There was a sharp increase in the number of businesses from 182 in 1960 to 355 in 1962. Moreover, Hurst Boulevard and Pipeline neared their development limits, and in the 1960s the town center moved northward. The movement was also stimulated in 1963 by the state's decision to build a new freeway on the north side connecting Fort Worth with Hurst. Bell Helicopter employed over 5,900 workers by the middle of the 1960s, far more than any other business in HEB. The Northeast campus of Tarrant County Junior College on the western edge of town stimulated still more population growth and jobs after opening in 1968. The town maintained a growth rate of over 10 percent annually in the 1960s and registered 27,215 in the 1970 census.

The burgeoning growth triggered occasional political tensions. In 1964 city councilman and former mayor, W. E. Vincent, was outraged at the city's decision to erect drainage structures along Lorean Branch on his and his partners' valuable property. Once Vincent allegedly stood guard there with a shotgun, on the northeast corner of Precinct Line and Bedford-Euless Road, to prevent the city from surveying his land. When the property was condemned by the city, Vincent persuaded District Judge Harold Craik to issue an injunction temporarily forbidding Hurst's construction of the culverts. The judge supposedly believed that condemnation required state legislation. City Attorney Tom Cave assured Mayor Fred Sturm and City Manager Don Edmonds that the judge had no jurisdiction. Rather than pay the construction company a ruinous thousand dollars a day to sit idle while the case was resolved, Sturm and Edmonds allowed the construction to proceed. Judge Craik found them in contempt of court. Upon refusing to pay their one-hundred dollar fines, the mayor and city manager of Hurst were arrested and put in jail on April 21st! They were not actually placed in cells, but they were fingerprinted and incarcerated behind six electronically-controlled doors. Cave secured their release in a few hours, but Sturm and Edmonds never forgot their "jailbird" time.

City elections were held in the midst of the dispute. Sturm was retiring and planning to leave the country, but citizens launched a write-in campaign for him against W. E. Vincent. Sturm — without campaigning — collected enough votes, 257, to force a runoff between developer Herman Smith, 320 votes, and incumbent Vincent, 284. Smith trounced Vincent in the runoff for city council, place 3. In July 1964, the Texas Supreme Court set aside the contempt decision issued by Judge Craik.

Euless also boomed, but first had to endure an episode that generated far more spectacular headlines than those in Hurst. In August 1949, without consulting anyone in Mosier Valley, Euless School Superintendent O. B. Powell contracted for the transfer of forty-six black students (including twelve from Hurst) to three "colored" schools in Fort Worth. Several other Tarrant County towns already followed the practice. Powell believed that busing would be cheaper than maintaining the black school in the long run and that Fort Worth schools would provide far better educational advantages than the tattered Mosier Valley facility. But in October the parents of fourteen school children living in Mosier Valley filed suit in U.S. District Court to enjoin the Euless school district from requiring black children to attend Fort Worth schools while schools for whites were maintained in Euless. The people of Mosier Valley boycotted the bus that was provided for the thirty-two-mile round trip and set up a private school in their Baptist Church.

Powell angrily charged that agitation by the National Association for the Advancement of Colored People led to the filing of the suit, which was true enough. His additional claim that, "The Negro people out here hardly know what the whole

thing is about" was wishful thinking. Over a hundred supportive Mosier Valley folks filled the courtroom for the opening-day testimony. Horace Coffee and Willie Parker, among other long-time residents of the community, testified that they had met in August and agreed not to allow their school children to be bused out of the district.

In June 1950, Judge Joe Dooley observed that the Fort Worth courses for "Negroes" probably excelled those in the Euless School for whites, but he ruled that Texas statutes expressly provided that students have the right to be educated in their own district and that a district's schools were supposed to be funded on an equal and impartial basis. He noted that $55,000 in public bond proceeds had recently been spent on the white school compared to about $1,500 for the Mosier Valley school.

Texas — with 1,100 districts that bused blacks to other districts — seemingly faced a new financial burden unless the decision could be successfully appealed. Powell warned that "Euless couldn't fight the battle for Texas and the South by itself." There was talk in the village that Euless or its school district might be annexed by Fort Worth, but Powell and the village school board called for the passage of a $25,000 bond issue dedicated mostly to the black school.

On the eve of the election, with a few repairs having begun at the school, the facility was vandalized. Powell personally urged blacks to vote in the August bond election, which about sixteen did, but a white backlash defeated the bond 101 to 57. Suddenly on the morning of September 4, 1950, thirty-five black grade-school students, their parents, and NAACP spokesmen entered the Euless School shortly after 8:00 A.M. and demanded enrollment along with white pupils. Word quickly spread throughout town and a resentful crowd of some 150 white residents, a few of whom were apparently armed, gathered outside on the school grounds during the two hours in which Powell addressed the black delegation in the school auditorium. Outside there were angry denunciations of the blacks, but the only violence was directed toward the media. A *Fort Worth Press* photographer was hit in the face and his camera seized, a black photographer was relieved of his camera, and the WBAP-TV reporter was warned to turn his television camera off. Powell consulted the hastily assembled school board, then informed the black delegation that he had to enforce the state segregation law. The blacks quietly filed out of the school, amidst white jeers, and enrolled at Mosier Valley.

Repairs then began in earnest at the black school – lights, water, and butane gas were provided, desks and paint added, and new outdoor toilets dug. The NAACP meanwhile backed away from the Euless case and in July 1951, the U.S. 5th Circuit Court of Appeals reversed Dooley's decision. A new brick school was completed in 1953 in Mosier Valley. (Mosier Valley was growing in the early 1950s. Black workers were attracted to construction jobs at Amon Carter Field and the Bell Helicopter plant. The population may have numbered 300.)

The civil rights activity in Euless was part of a series of incidents and cases in the 1940s and 1950s that culminated in the Brown ruling by the U.S. Supreme Court in 1954, ordering the desegregation of the nation's public schools with all deliberate speed. Most Texas districts resisted for years. The first integrated classes in the merged HEB district began in the summer of 1965 with a federal Head Start program. In the spring of 1968 the federal government threatened to cut off aid to the HEB school district unless the Mosier Valley facility was closed or integrated. It closed.

Euless had another problem by 1950 – most of the water wells were too shallow and had too much iron. And people who wanted to build homes couldn't secure FHA loans unless there was a water system, which required incorporation. Warren Fuller served as ex-officio mayor while initiating proceedings for incorporation and a water supply in 1950. Then he was elected the first mayor when the village incorporated, apparently in April 1951. Euless barely scraped up the requisite 110 water tie-ins for every domicile and store in town and obtained a water supply several weeks ahead of Hurst. Homer Fuller succeeded his brother as mayor in the summer of 1951. Sometime in 1952 some residents were sufficiently irate over water and sewer taxes that the town narrowly voted to disincorporate. Several dissidents were carved out of the city limits and the villagers voted again to incorporate on February 24, 1953.

Public services were enhanced. The Euless post office was revived in February 1949, in a corner of Fullers' grocery. New grocery co-owner Robert Nail switched hats between grocer and postmaster until the postal position eventually took precedence. Fire fighting abilities improved when a local rancher donated a fire truck, which was loaded with $1,200 in equipment provided by

the county. In the summer of 1951 the truck was manned by a handful of volunteers and assigned to fighting grass fires in the area. A police department was created in 1957 with W. M. "Blackie" Sustaire as the first chief. He operated out of the fire station-city hall building on present Highway 10, near Main Street. Sustaire often slept by the radio on a cot in the station so he could respond to emergencies. In 1964 the fire department began changing from a volunteer organization by hiring permanent personnel (two drivers). The Euless Lions Club organized in the 1950s and took the lead in creating a city library in 1961. With fewer than 3,000 books, it was housed in a converted one-car garage on Fuller Drive across the street from the post office.

Like Hurst, Euless directly benefited from the 1953 openings of Bell Helicopter and Amon Carter Field as well as the paving of Farm-to-Market Road 157 and State Highway 183 (now 10). In 1957 the Western Hills Inn was built at the intersection of 157 and old 183, where it is still in business. It housed the Chamber of Commerce from 1958 to 1980. The American Airlines stewardess college, the first such institution in the country, was erected on the western edge of Carter Field. The million dollar installation was dedicated in November 1957 by Speaker of the House, Sam Rayburn. Bill Byers, who had helped build the Euless Lumber Company over a decade before, became manager in 1956 and later bought it. His business at 200 West Euless Boulevard is the oldest continuing one in town. Some enterprises, of course, were founded on a shoestring but grew to prosperity with the town. In 1958 William Hay borrowed $300 to launch a printing business in Fort Worth, which he moved to Hurst in 1959 and to Euless in the early 1960s. The Hurst-Euless Printing Company expanded to an 8,000 square-foot site and has done much of the printing for HEB businesses and institutions over the years.

Some businesses vanished or had to change their operations because of the growth process. Improved highways forced local dairies to compete with some that were farther away. And many local dairies were on leased lands, which were sold out from under them by developers. Tennessee Dairies in downtown Euless closed in the mid-1950s. Outlying dairies, e.g. those north of Euless owned by John and Joe Fitch and by Leo Savage and one east of town owned by Clark Smith, lasted through the 1970s and early 1980s before development caught up with them. James P. Jones, who settled there in 1957 and became the only veternarian in HEB at the time, recollects that some 15 percent of his initial business was handling dairy cows and farm horses. That segment of his enterprise shrank to virtually nothing by the end of the 1970s.

Old-line churches grew spectacularly, and new ones were organized in people's homes. The Baptists split again in 1956, but both churches grew; the construction of First Baptist's current complex on Airport Freeway began in 1964. First Methodist built its present sanctuary in 1960. St. Vincent's Episcopal was established in Jess Holder's home in Hurst in 1955. By 1960 it was a self-supporting parish with 120 members, and a church was erected that year on Pipeline Road in Euless. The Euless First Assembly of God began with eight adults in 1956 in the home of Earl Pendergrass, who served as pastor for sixteen years. It had 150 members within three months and in 1960 erected a new building at South Main and Whitener.

Warren Fuller had abandoned his general store in 1958 and was dabbling in real estate when Dallas developer Carr Collins stopped by his office during a thunderstorm. Collins wanted to see some pieces of land immediately. The two looked at innumerable tracts that people wanted to sell, amounting to about 600 acres at about $1,500 an acre. Once back at Fuller's office, Collins still hadn't reacted to Fuller's salesmanship, but the Dallas magnate suddenly blurted, "I got things to do. I'll take it." A bit confused, Fuller asked, "What piece do you want?" Collins retorted, "All of it — fix up the papers," and walked out the door. "It was close to a million dollar deal," Fuller remembers, "and it was the start of Euless." This was the Midway Park development north and west of the old First Baptist Church. Collins built twenty-five or thirty homes, offered a special deal on radio and TV one Sunday, and sold them all in a single afternoon. They sold for less than $7,500 each, with monthly payments less than $65. Herman Smith was another real estate entrepreneur who invested heavily and eventually developed the 500-home Wilshire subdivision in southeast Euless in the 1960s. The first of the Sotogrande luxury apartments was built in 1969.

Euless' population surged from about 300 in 1950 to 4,236 in 1960. The population continued increasing dramatically in the early 1960s, when for three straight years Euless was the state's fastest growing city. It had the highest growth rate in the county, 340 percent in the 1960s. By 1970 the census recorded 19,316 people and 130 business establishments.

In 1961 Mayor W. G. Fuller (no kin to the other Fullers) and the city council adopted a home rule charter, approved by the voters, 128 to 38. The first bond election for city improvements, 1964, put over $3,000,000 into streets, drainage, parks, and a city hall/community center (completed at 201 Ector Drive in 1966). The center housed the police department and the library. In 1965 another $5,500,000 in revenue bonds allowed the city to buy the Euless-Bedford water-sewer system. The city complex continues to provide Euless with much of its modern identity in the mid-cities.

Urban problems reach out to the suburbs, of course, as dramatically illustrated in Euless in 1967. At 9:00 A.M. on October 7 three young men staged a holdup in commando fashion wearing grotesque Halloween masks, but they ran into the police and an agile customer who wrested one bandit's pistol away from him. The *Dallas Times-Herald* summed it up, "A bandit was slain with his own gun, another was killed by police gunfire, and two customers were wounded Saturday night in a blazing shootout at Buddie's Supermarket in Euless."

A bit more removed from the action, Bedford did not grow at the same pace as Hurst and Euless in the 1950s, which perhaps lent false encouragement to old-line families that they might stave off complete urbanization. The village's post office was reestablished in June 1950, with Postmaster Walter Fitch operating it in his store. The first great stimulus to growth after the war occurred in 1949 when the theatrical Variety Club of Dallas purchased a 232-acre tract northwest of the business district and established Boys Ranch. With two brick dormitories and a gym, it was a home for troubled boys, ages ten to fourteen; it began with some fifty boys and increased to about one hundred early in 1953.

In fear of being swallowed up by Euless or Hurst, Bedford voted to incorporate, 55 to 20, on January 22, 1953. Its population was a little over 400 within a two square mile area, counting the boys and personnel at Boys' Ranch. David Sloan was the first mayor.

Signs of growth began to appear. The Murphy and Belhurst additions were launched in the early 1950s. Herman's Washateria featured artesian water and a six cent wash. Joe Welborn began an electrical and appliance repair shop. The volunteer firefighters had no equipment and just fought fires with sacks, but, upon organizing in 1955, they purchased surplus army trucks and — after hours in Bilger's garage — rebuilt them into fire fighting engines. Residents donated some $4,000 toward the cost of a $15,000 fire station/civic center. Fitch gave the land, and additional donations in labor and materials amounted to about half the total cost. One of the money-raising techniques of the time was the annual barbecue, where over a thousand usually attended and Bedford Road would be roped off. Community spirit was high when the center was built, next to the old well, in 1958. There were already indications that Bedford was determined to follow an independent course. As talk of merging schools arose, many townfolk believed that the other two cities were only interested in their money. School merger was at first voted down in Bedford in the mid-1950s.

Bedford was also shoved toward insularity by Hurst. At the tumultuous 1957 meeting of the officials from thirteen towns, at which Hurst Mayor W. E. Vincent briefly presided, it was apparent that the chief contention for territory was between Hurst and Bedford. One strip included in Hurst's annexation ordinance had been annexed by Bedford six months earlier. After Vincent asserted that Hurst was not grabbing land, but just trying to protect everyone's interests, he was bombarded with a wave of moans. Mayor Sloan shouted, "How does that shoe taste by now? You've had it in your mouth all night." When Vincent refused to back down, Sloan proclaimed, "That's all I wanted to know" and walked out. The meeting abruptly broke up.

School district mergers commenced despite the inter-village squabbles. The Hurst and Euless districts merged in 1955. That year $600,000 in bonds were voted, and the new L. D. Bell High School at Pipeline and Raider (present Central Jr. High School) was completed in January 1957. Several of the old families in Euless were outraged that even though Euless harbored the only heritage of a high school in the district, the first high school was built in Hurst. For a time Euless had no members on the board. In the first two years district enrollment leaped from about 1,400 students to almost 2,300.

Remarkably, Bedford voted to join the district in November 1958, by a vote of 212 to 189, and when consolidation became effective in 1959 the HEB district numbered some 3,965 students and 156 teachers. Six schools were built off the same set of prints; three new schools or large portions of them opened just in 1960. Overcrowding was so bad that parents at West Hurst Elementary petitioned for the busing of their children fifteen miles to Euless, but instead portable buildings were purchased. Overcrowding forced Bell to move to its present Brown Trail location in 1966. Trinity High School opened in 1969 with some 1,200 students. Over 12,000 students were added in the 1960s and so were such urban phenomena as sex education classes and a dress code that allowed girls to wear slacks when it was freezing. The district was a pioneer builder of the so-called carousel schools in 1967. Midway Park Elementary in Euless was the first of these round buildings, people-centered schools featuring light, color, full-wall bulletin-display centers, and trapezoidal shaped classrooms, no two exactly alike.

On one occasion the school district misjudged the rising public resentment against the ever-expanding costs of government. The district touted a $4,500,000 bond issue in 1968. A week before the bond election the school board announced — with a stupefying lack of timing — that a school tax increase of some 7 to 12 percent would soon be necessary. Independent School District officials pointed out that the tax increase was not related to the bonds, which were for construction and improvements. The Hurst-Euless Chamber of Commerce did not get around to endorsing the bonds until the day of the election. Voters defeated the bond issue, 620 to 424. A number of them were heard to say, as they were leaving the polls, that they had no chance to vote against various sales and surtaxes, "but here's one we can vote against."

Meanwhile, between 1955 and 1960 Bedford's area increased almost 400 percent in about forty separate annexations. The 1960 census showed the town with 2,706 people within ten square miles. Innumerable housing developments caused Bedford to grow over 13 percent annually in the 1960s and register a population of 10,049 in 1970. Many long-time settlers, unable to pay school district and county taxes, had to sell some of their land to developers and speculators. Developers complained that their rezoning requests languished and the land prices they paid were outrageous. In Bedford's tumultuous year of 1966 the town led the county in percentage of businesses gained that year; the total rose from twenty-two to thirty-one. It was a breathtaking pace.

The most spectacular single development was undoubtedly Stonegate. Tom Purvis and Jack York built some 300 houses along Bedford Road, just east of Brown Trail, with a British motif. Distinctive architecture, huge antique British lampposts, Stony the lion, and large, colorful street signs in the shapes of coats of arms were among the attractions that lured some 20,000 to the opening day in April 1960.

A *Fort Worth Star-Telegram* writer described Bedford early in 1963 as a "Happy 'Bedroom' Suburb Town Without Taxation," governed mostly by residents who had deep historical roots in the community — Mayor U. Z. (Easy) Jernigan, who conducted the first meetings with a gavel on an apple box, City Secretary Walter Fitch, and two elected commissioners, builder Raymond McManus and mechanical engineer William Wolf. Only Wolf was a recent arrival. The "taxless utopia" was financed by about $9,000 annually (by 1963) from developers' plat fees and building permits and franchise payments from utility companies.

Before the year was out, however, a voluntary system of paying for a town patrolman had ended in failure and heavier and heavier traffic on Bedford's streets began to take its toll in chug holes. The population was about 4,000. Many newcomers became convinced that the leadership provided by Bedford's historic families was unable to make the transition from a rural to an urban community. Geologist Will Clack and other dissidents called for enhanced city services and an independent audit of the town's financial records, among other demands. As town clerk, Fitch spent innumerable hours writing out building permits and such, and took this occasion to resign after a decade at a nonpaying job. He asked for an audit of his own books before some 125 townspeople at the November 11th council meeting. Applause came from both sides.

Some street improvements were made in 1964, a zoning ordinance was passed, and a small library with 1,500 books was established in a former residence, but no town police protection or taxation was attempted. Additional complaints accumulated concerning the lack of a parks and recreation board, inadequate water pressure, and some streets being beyond repair. Yet in 1964 and 1965 the town twice voted down the newcomers' efforts to obtain a home rule charter in place of general law. Since both factions wanted more representation in running the town, Bedford did change its form of government in May 1965, from a two-man commission to a five-person aldermanic type. Several full-time city staff were hired.

Finally in October Mayor Jernigan and the council unanimously called upon Bedford to approve a $5,000,000 bond election for water, sewers, and streets. A proposed tax rate of sixty cents per $100 assessed valuation would pay off the bonds. Bedfordites were "shaken considerably" and voted down all five propositions, but the stunned mayor and aldermen carefully presented their case again in January with a $4,000,000 proposal and it passed comfortably. Yet the bonds proved difficult to sell during the political disarray.

The bickering over taxation led to bitter divisiveness in city elections. For months Bedford police had to escort councilmen and mayors in and out of disorderly meetings in the old fire hall. Wolf challenged Jernigan for mayor in April 1966 and edged him by an announced margin of 353 to 337. Four aldermen refused to accept Wolf and declared the mayor's post vacant due to irregularities. One complaint was that Wolf had not filed the required campaign expense statement, but neither had some of the aldermen who called a second mayoralty election. Wolf took his case to Judge Walter Jordan's 48th District Court, which upheld him.

Meanwhile, the "old Bedford" aldermen had selected a fifteen-person charter commission (in order to stave off an elected charter commission) to draw up a home rule charter. But Mayor Wolf promptly answered a petition and set July 9, 1966, as the date for a special election on a home rule charter. On the eve of the balloting Wolf removed three aldermen who refused to recognize the election. Bedford approved the home rule charter 304 to 222 and, from among thirty-one candidates, elected fifteen persons, mostly supporters of the mayor. This second commission also began to draft a charter.

The aldermen hauled Wolf to court. Speaking to some fifty Bedford residents in his courtroom, Judge Jordan informed Mayor Wolf, "You had no more right to get rid of the aldermen than they did to keep you out of office." The judge also observed that the discord was giving Bedford "a bad name." Two months later the judge ruled that state law did not permit the mayor alone to call a charter commission election. The ruling cleared the way for the September 24th election (the fifth election of the year) for a vote on the charter being drawn up by the commission selected by the aldermen. Wolf and most of his backers were outraged, particularly since the proposed charter allowed the incumbent aldermen to retain their positions until an April 1968 election. The home rule charter and council-manager government were adopted, 388 to 309, but no city manager was hired because of the political chaos.

In the midst of the turmoil in July 1966, Bedford resident W. R. Petty, minister of the Church of Christ in Euless, secured 162 signatures on another petition — to abolish Bedford and have it annexed by Euless. Angry Bedford councilmen refused to call an election on various pretexts, but in October Judge Jordan, arbitrating his fourth Bedford dispute within a year, ordered the town to hold a merger election. Euless also set an election. The councilmen appealed and drug out the case until spring, but lost again.

When amalgamation was discussed in 1966 realtor Herman Smith, former mayor of Hurst, observed that the merger of all three towns might be necessary. As primarily residential communities, they might have to economize — by avoiding duplication of city departments — "in order not to tax our residences right out of existence." Smith also noted that a merged HEB would give it a more important voice in the Dallas-Fort Worth region and would allow the area to plan more effectively for future expansion. Mayor Wolf also believed that Hurst, Euless, and Bedford were destined to become one large community anyway, and that merger made good economic sense for all three. Mayor Fuller was not ready to take on Hurst, but he and Wolf took the lead in the Euless-Bedford merger drive.

By the spring of 1967 the specific arguments for merger in Bedford were that residents would receive a water and sewer system (already owned by Euless), a new complex of municipal buildings, and various city services that were deficient in Bedford. The town's proponents of merger, led by Mayor Wolf and former Mayor E. C. Hardisty, also argued that Bedford's property tax rate of sixty cents per $100 of vaulation could not pay for the development of the city. When the $4,000,000 bonds approved in 1966 were sold, taxes would have to rise to at least ninety cents or up to $1.40 to retire the bonds. The Euless rate of .77 per $100 valuation, after being extended to the combined city, would probably survive four or five years without additional tax cost to the citizens of either area. Moreover, a stable city government would result and the united city would rank fourth in size in Tarrant County and would have a more prominent voice in county and state affairs.

The opposition's arguments were that taxes would rise immediately over 28 percent, that they were retroactive to January 1st, and that each Bedford family would be burdened with an average $1,420 share of Euless' $9,500,000 debt. Moreover, Euless would apparently dominate Bedford on the city council by five to two, assuming that Euless actually agreed to enlarge its council from five members to seven. Bedford, it was pointed out, was debt-free and had the lowest tax rates in the area. Don Brown and the Bedford Homeowners Association, with the assistance of a public relations firm (hired by Fitch), packaged and distributed its message more widely and effectively than the proponents of merger. The Fitches owned millions of dollars worth of land in Bedford, but the old-line families were perhaps as concerned with their sense of community as with the alleged economic liabilities of merger. Old-time residents of Bedford and Euless were the most skeptical, and those in Bedford, which had a population of some 6,000 at the time, often cited fears of being swallowed up and ignored by Euless, whose population was around 12,000. Evelyn Fitch noted at the June 15th public meeting, where the shouting almost got out of hand, that Euless would dictate the name of the new city, and that one Euless councilman had suggested "Bedless" or "Euford." Mayor Fuller replied that the suggestion had been a jest, but it was clearly a badly-timed joke. Postmaster Walter Fitch summed it up for old Bedford, "My heritage, my life, my all is in this town."

Actually, in all probability the tax could not legally be retroactive. Bedford residents were already paying on Euless revenue bonds through the water and sewer system, and not all of the $9,500,000 in bonds had been issued at the time. The merged council, whatever its size, would all be elected at large, and any name change would be put to a general vote — but, of course, Euless had more voters.

Euless property owners were promised by proponents that they would stand to gain materially through increased land values due to the general expansion of the city and would realize savings through sharing the cost of city government. Euless, as the dominant partner, was not caught up in the merger issue. The election hinged on the opponents' economic arguments, which persuaded a crucial number of relatively recent arrivals in Bedford to keep the town intact. In a record 60 percent turnout of the registered voters, June 24, 1967, Bedford rejected the merger, 975 to 422. In a 16 percent turnout, Euless approved it, 211 to 133, but amalgamation required the approval of both towns. Two days after the election Mayor Wolf announced he would not run again. Two years later his successor announced a tax hike to .85 per $100 valuation.

Bedford was one of several suburban towns in Tarrant County that experienced political growing pains in the 1960s. The earlier Euless incorporation battle apparently was similar but occurred on a smaller scale and without any newspaper coverage. One cause of the volatile politics was the reluctance of many, especially the old-line families reared in the countryside, to pay city taxes — yet virtually all residents were discontented with the second-rate services. There were also personality conflicts — some leaders found it difficult to compromise and to cope with large numbers of new people and their ideas; this was true for some suburbanites encountering countryside leaders as well as vice-versa. Both causes were exacerbated in smaller communities like Euless and Bedford that had not yet hired a city staff, especially a city manager. Too often councilmen were untrained in municipal affairs, groping for expert information and legal advice, and faced with conflicting facts and opinions on the same issue.

Shortly after the merger fiasco and Mayor Wolf's retirement, Bedford resumed the movement toward partial integration of the tri-cities area that had begun in 1958 in the school system. The Bedford Chamber of Commerce merged with the Hurst-Euless Chamber in 1969, which it could effect only after Walter Fitch retired as chairman. That same year the three cities agreed to establish a hospital district and started fund-raising for a community facility to be located in Bedford. The Bedford School closed in 1969, severing another link with the town's independent past.

As the suburbs grew, old-line residents and area scholars also became conscious of the need to unite in efforts to collect the reminiscences of veteran settlers and to preserve treasured historical sites. The Mid-Cities Historical Society was launched in the early 1960s. Mrs. Frank Estill, Evelyn Fitch, Weldon Cannon, and Dodie Souder, representing all three communities, provided much of the impetus. Its efforts merged with those of educators Duane Gage and Mike Patterson, who researched several HEB sites which were subsequently designated with Texas Historical Markers. And Gage established the Heritage Room at TCJC, for the preservation of Northeast Tarrant County records and reminiscences. Also, the Hurst Art Association was organized in 1961 to promote community interest in the fine arts. It was renamed the Trinity Arts Guild in 1968 and attracted participants from Euless and Bedford as well as Hurst. Merger of the towns had failed, but cooperative endeavors were succeeding.

1966. Bedford citizens worked nights and weekends in 1957 to build their town offices. For the first seven years town council meetings were peaceable and sparsely attended, but from 1964 through 1967 the community center was the site of spirited and fractious debates over city services, a contested mayorality election, a disputed home rule charter, and the contentious question of abolishing the town of Bedford and merging with Euless. By this time a larger city hall was needed. — Courtesy of Fort Worth Star-Telegram Photograph Collection, Special Collections Division, University of Texas at Arlington Libraries

ca. 1950. By 1950 Highway 183 (formerly Highway 15 and now designated as Highway 10) was upgraded and waiting for the urbanization of Hurst and Euless to begin. Here truckers on the route between Dallas and Fort Worth found a welcome rest stop at Midge's Cafe across the street from Hurst Public School. — Courtesy Tarrant County Junior College

1954. Looking south on Precinct Line Road at the Bedford-Euless Road intersection in Hurst, one sees the site of one of the Hurst Police Department's first accident investigations. Today at the intersection there is an automobile agency, a service station, a lubication service, and a funeral home. — Courtesy Hurst Police Department

1975. Looking north on Norwood Drive at West Hurst Boulevard, one may see the nature of Hurst's commercial development in the 1950s--modest structures scattered along a main road, only two or three structures per block. The old tin building once housed the city's first fire truck. — Courtesy Lee Switzer

1950. The old Mosier Valley School for blacks, some or all of which probably dated back to 1918, lacked water, screens, and the simplest amenities. Repairs and such facilities as new outdoor toilets commenced immediately after blacks tried to integrate the Euless white school in September 1950. The refurbished school now stands in old downtown Bedford.
— Courtesy *Fort Worth Star-Telegram* Photograph Collection, Special Collections Division,
University of Texas at Arlington Libraries

1950. A tense crowd gathers outside the Euless School auditorium on the morning of September 4th, 1950, after blacks from Mosier Valley attempted to enroll their children there. Superintendent O. B. Powell was inside, addressing the black delegation. Blacks were denied entry, but extensive repairs began immediately on the Mosier Valley School. L. G. Spencer, wearing hat, is in the right foreground of the picture, talking to Luther Morelock. Second from the right, near the right corner of the building, is Emmitt Himes. Near the center of the picture, under the light, with hand in pocket, is Hubert Fuller. — Courtesy *Fort Worth Star-Telegram* Photograph Collection, Special Collections Division, University of Texas at Arlington Libraries

ca. 1956. A Fuller family photograph shows the five brothers, on the front row from the left--Warren, Andrew, Larkin, Ed, and Homer. The ladies from the left are Callie (Fuller) Whitener, Essie (Weatherly) Fuller, Edna (Fuller) Deacon, Virginia (Payton) Fuller, and Ruth (Fuller) Millican. All remained in Euless except Larkin, who moved to Dallas, and Edna, who moved to Panhandle, Texas. — Courtesy Troy Fuller

1965. Integration began in the HEB School District in the summer of 1965, with a Head Start class that included children from Mosier Valley and a black teacher, Vada Johnson, who was a teacher in the Mosier Valley School. A descendant of Mosier Valley freedmen, Vada Johnson became the first black school teacher in HEB and in 1976 was acclaimed as Teacher of the Year in the district. — Courtesy Tarrant County Junior College

1991. Looking north from Airport Freeway, Euless' city complex has the appearance of a spacious campus.
— Courtesy Duane Gage

ca. 1950. There was a reassuring continuity in Fitch's General Merchandise Store in Bedford. Proprietor Walter Finch, descendant of Bedford founder Weldon Bobo, operated the store from 1933 to 1963, extending the family's operation of the store to ninety years. The site of community picnics, local elections, gasoline pump, and rural mail exchange, Fitch's was the social center of the village. Here Walter and wife Evelyn (right) are assisted by local resident Mrs. Mayfield in setting up a display of Swift's products. – Courtesy Evelyn Fitch-George

1964. Looking east along Bedford Road in "downtown" Bedford in 1964, one sees a small village seemingly oblivious to the rapid urban growth swirling around it. – Courtesy Tarrant County Junior College

1965. The Fort Worth Press *reported that fourteen Bedford firemen earned ten-year service pins, including, from the left, Jack Mayfield, Oather Gardner, T. J. Mayfield, Ed Bilger, Sr., Chief L. L. "Smokey" Hines, R. E. McManus, Gerhard Laczny, and James Simmons. Not on hand for the photo were E. M. Bilger, Jr., John Martin, Curtis McCaffity, Donald Geer, Tom Acton, and Walter Finch. — Courtesy Mr. and Mrs. Ed Bilger and Mr. and Mrs. Ed Bilger, Jr.*

ca. 1968. Bill Wolf, on left, the first outsider to become mayor of Bedford (April 1966), fought for establishing a home rule charter, hiring a city manager, and merging Bedford with Euless. Shown here beside Wolf is Euless Mayor William G. Fuller and Hurst Mayor Russell Johnson, on right, attending a Democratic party rally for Texas Lt. Gov. Ben Barnes. Affluent new arrivals moving into these cities would soon make northeast Tarrant County heavily Republican.

– Courtesy W. D. Smith, Inc., and Patricia Wolf Garza

1975. Meeting in the Heritage Room in TCJC's Library to promote the preservation of northeast Tarrant County's historic photographs, documents, and memorabilia are, left to right, Jeanette Tingle, Duane Gage, Weldon Cannon, Zane Fields, Estelle Teague, Dulce Moore, Dr. Herman Crow (Northeast Campus President), Tommye Osburn, Jane McCray, Ruth Wickam, and Thelma Ray. The Heritage Room Collection includes hundreds of student research papers on local history topics. – Courtesy Tarrant County Junior College

1970s. In the 1920s and 1930s the largest employer in the HEB area was the Fort Worth Sand and Gravel Company. Operating between the Trinity River and the Rock Island Railway, it and successor companies have provided a major portion of the Dallas-Fort Worth area's construction materials since the early 1920s. – Courtesy Tarrant County Junior College

1974. The new Hurst-Euless Printing Company building stands at what is now l0720 South Pipeline Road. William Hay started his printing business in Fort Worth in 1958, moved to Hurst in 1959 and adopted the town's name for his company, and moved again (and expanded) in the early 1960s to 201 Raider and changed the name to Hurst-Euless Printing Company. Printing materials for other businesses, it quickly outgrew its 2,000 square feet and moved into its present building in 1966. Its 5,000 square feet were enlarged an additional 3,000 square feet in 1974. Hay's first partner was Bob Taylor, succeeded by Mack W. Hopkins in 1961. Hopkins died in 1973. Bobby Bryant began working for the company in 1965 and bought into it in 1971 to become co-owner and vice-president. In 1974 Michael Hay, William's son, went to work for the company and in 1985 became a third owner and a vice-president. — Courtesy Hurst-Euless Printing Company

ca. 1956. Hurst developed a volunteer fire department in the 1950s. Here E. O. Kaiser, J. F. Van Wyckhouse, Ollie Dunn, Keith Robinson, and C. K. Lykins are checking out a new fire truck. The department received its first resuscitator in 1958.
— Courtesy Tarrant County Junior College

1973. When the Dallas-Fort Worth Airport opened in 1974 it created thousands of jobs, stimulated numerous relocations, and spurred intensive speculative real estate investment. This construction scene in 1973 shows the sprawling facility encompassing dozens of homestead sites on Grapevine Prairie. – Courtesy Dallas-Fort Worth International Airport

V. The Maturing Towns, 1970s–1990s

Hurst was the first of the tri-cities to settle into the mode of a bustling, expanding town. Traditional community gathering places died in the suburbanizing process, but new ones were born. Emma Souder abandoned the cafe business in 1949, closed her grocery store after seventeen years in 1953, and went to work for the city. When C. A. and Gwen Sanford opened C.A.'s Restaurant in May 1962, at 440 West Pipeline Road, it was one of the few sit-down diners in the area. Coffee was five cents, hamburgers forty-five cents. An unpaved Pipeline Road was supplanting old 183 as the main street, and there were no homes north of Pipeline. After becoming a local hotbed for politics and establishing a nationwide reputation for chicken-fried steaks, C.A.'s closed twenty-five years later in 1987.

The population in the 1960s and 1970s shifted northward from its first belt of settlement along old Highway 183 to such streets as Bedford-Euless Road, and it shifted from primarily blue-collar to white-collar. Professionals, with their higher incomes, sought big lots and small town atmosphere in their desire to escape Dallas and Fort Worth. A goodly number were northerners and Republicans. In pursuit of these newcomers' upper middle class incomes were service businesses and retailers. After fears surfaced that the growth would rage out of control, a Citizens Resource Panel for Planning was assembled in Hurst and reported in 1971 that the town's first goal should be to prevent population density from ever reaching 7.6 people per acre. Growth was certainly not "controlled," but the 1970s and 1980s in Hurst were more noted for the retail onslaught than burgeoning population. Northeast

Mall arrived in 1972 at the crossroads of Airport Freeway and Loop 820. The mall doubled Hurst's retail sales the month it opened. Hurst's retail sales during 1973 were $79,000,000, while Euless' were $18,000,000 and Bedford's $4,000,000. (After three renovations, Northeast Mall remains the largest shopping center in Tarrant County.)

In addition the roar of the first jets touching down at the Dallas-Fort Worth Airport, January 1974, signaled a speculative land rush that also seemed to benefit Hurst most of all. Developers declined to pay $10,000 to $15,000 an acre in Euless when they could acquire it for $3,000 to $4,000 in Hurst. Small developers were the norm in Hurst, and typical elsewhere in HEB, because of the small farm ownership pattern and because of the character of the land — the innumerable trees and ravines made drainage a mess. Large operators prefer flat, treeless plains. Given the prosperity of the residents in the 1970s and the desire to place some limits on growth, Hurst adopted stricter building codes and maintained better services than its sister cities. The population increased to 31,400 in 1980. The opening of North Hills Mall, 1979, provided additional shopping facilities for Hurst and the growing northeastern quadrant of the county.

The skidding economy of the early 1980s was the first outside event that limited Hurst's development. Its hotspot location in the mid-cities was no longer sufficient to insure economic development. By 1981, the year the town became landlocked, some 85 percent of Hurst was already developed anyway.

Floods in the early 1980s forced Hurst to expend considerable money on drainage improvements. By the 1970s and 1980s the third belt of settlement, including restaurants, shopping centers, and hospitals in Hurst (and Bedford), provide a more urban atmosphere along Airport Freeway. By the 1980s the freeway seemed to split Hurst between its prosperous northern half and its not so prosperous southern section.

Change runs amok in modern urban and suburban America and no sooner had the town achieved a professional, white collar ambiance than it had to turn its attention to the quality of life and improving the older areas of the community. In 1983 Mayor Bill Souder and the city council required developers of multifamily housing to provide amenities such as trees, masonry fences, and other extras to qualify for increased density. In 1983 for the first time tax revenue from commercial establishments such as malls and shopping centers surpassed tax revenues from homeowners. Faced with a fluctuating economy and no room to expand, the city made the transition in the 1980s to a limited-growth mode, and it matured and become an active competitor for commercial sites. By the end of the decade Hurst had some seventeen parks, a fairly high number for a town of its size. Hurst slipped from first to third in population among the tri-cities; the 1990 count showed the town with fewer than 33,600 people. With the virtual buildout of the town in 1990, the density was 5.5 people per acre.

The desire to limit growth and preserve a certain quality of life, of course, clashed with the desire to continue developing economically, to attract tax-paying entities that help finance vital services. There was an ongoing struggle in the planning and zoning board in the 1960s and 1970s over the efforts of developers to build 150-foot deep shopping centers — which deteriorate more rapidly than malls — along Precinct Line and Pipeline Roads. In 1980 a group of irate residents in Hurst's Continental Addition, initially opposed to a shopping center at Melbourne Road and Cheryl, were so fed up with traffic congestion that they petitioned (unsuccessfully) for a two-year halt in commercial building. In the mid-1980s Hurst could have been the site for a Sam's store, which would have immediately generated some $500,000 in revenue per year, but the council believed that the proposed building was not a quality brick structure. Councilman Ralph Butts and others were also perturbed over the excessive traffic that would have been generated at the proposed site, the Precinct Line-Harwood intersec-

tion, across the street from the junior college. Sam's turned down other proposed Hurst sites and went to Richland Hills.

Problems with youths were part of the growth and suburbanization process, as in the rest of the nation. By 1970, after the teen canteen had faded away, teenagers from HEB and the metroplex were disturbing the Belaire Shopping Center, on the Hurst-Bedford boundary on Pipeline Road, with after-hours drinking, littering and drag racing. Hurst police discovered in the 1970s that when they ticketed the bumper-to-bumper cruisers who remained after the center's ten p.m. curfew, the problem would pop up elsewhere, such as at a nearby Piggly Wiggley grocery store. The police devised a tactic that worked — after police observers were certain that a particular car had repeatedly trespassed, the occupants were counseled in a friendly fashion that cruising prevented patrons from entering stores. For the moment, the driver's name was merely entered into a notebook, but he was warned that on the next occasion, criminal trespass charges would be filed against him. If that deterrent proved insufficient, the police promised to impound the car, which was done a few times. The more determined cruisers moved on to other metroplex sites. Many citizens felt that the cities had no obligation to spend tax money to provide entertainment for teenagers, but the new Hurst Civic Center and various churches absorbed some — but not enough — of the teen activity in the 1980s.

The town's largest employer, Bell Helicopter Textron, has been closely tied to defense contracts. During the height of the Vietnam War in the late 1960s, Bell's workforce topped 11,000, many of them assembling Hueys, but employment dropped below 7,000 in 1972 as the war wound down. By 1977, with a renewal of federal defense programs, Bell counted 12,000 employees. The company had built and delivered nearly 23,000 military and commercial helicopters, more than all other helicopter manufacturers combined. The maiden flight of the XV-15 tilt-rotor research aircraft also occurred in 1977. In the early 1980s Bell finished its major defense projects about the same time that energy companies stopped buying helicopters and the economy went into a tailspin. By 1983 Bell's employment was little more than 6,000, and the company became largely a spare parts maker. By 1988 the local plant was concentrating on the long-awaited V-22 Osprey tilt-rotor craft that the Marines wanted, but layoffs began in

1989 when federal funding became uncertain. Local Bell employment was about 7,000 in 1991, the fourth largest in the county, but would have plummeted if the Osprey had been eliminated from the federal budget. The company's Kiowa Warrior earned a deadly reputation as a scout helicopter in the Persian Gulf War, 1991, but its funding had also become tenuous. The 1992 contract to build Ospreys for the Marines staved off further layoffs and greatly benefited Bell's efforts to produce the V-22 for civilian use, but there are no long-term guarantees from either the defense or civilian sectors. There will be other contracts, but Bell, like other defense contractors, will probably have to slim down even more to remain competitive.

Hurst began sponsoring an annual art show in 1986, displaying local paintings rather than crafts. Several thousand usually attend the two-day event at Chisholm Park. In 1991 the city established the annual Very Special Arts Festival, noncompetitive crafts and sports at the Hurst Recreational Center for the physically and mentally challenged.

Darnell Hale's *Hurst Review* began in 1957, but the *Mid-Cities Daily News*, which originated in Fort Worth as a group of weekly advertising sheets, moved to Hurst by 1960 and dominated the HEB newspaper market. The owners, Stanley McBrayer and Jenkins Garrett, believed in the 1960s and 1970s that their greatest task was to curb the fighting between the old residents who resisted urbanization and the newcomers who were part of it. In that spirit — in addition to covering the local scene — the paper continues to sponsor gatherings that bring together community leaders, businessmen, and taxpaying citizens from the mid-cities. In the late 1970s the *Fort Worth Star-Telgram* opened a bureau with one reporter in Northeast Tarrant County. In 1988 it was expanded to an independent news-gathering arm with a full complement of reporters, photographers, and advertising representatives. They publish the Northeast Metropolitan edition of the *Star-Telegram*.

At the scene of most of the suburban fighting, Bedford, the town's 1961 master plan zoned everything as single-family or agricultural, but it was replaced by another plan with apartment zoning under Mayor Wolf in 1968. The plan predicted that Bedford would contain over 60,000 people by 1990, and that the football-shaped district carved by the freeways in the center of the community, between Bedford Road and 121, should be the central business district. Many houses were in this 500-acre district, however, and it was larger than downtown Dallas.

In 1970 Bedford city officials announced the imminent development of a 200-acre commercial strip on the east side of Central, north of State Highway 121; they announced the 700-acre Bedford Forum project, also on the east side, with apartments, motels, offices, and an industrial park; and they announced Sears' proposed 130-acre shopping center at Spur 350 and Central. A Dallas realtor planned to develop townhouses and a boutique shopping center while demolishing existing buildings at the old Bedford Boys Ranch, abandoned by the Variety Club in 1957 and used by churches for twelve years. In 1971, the year that the nearby American Airlines Flight Academy opened, a citizens group met with the city council and endorsed the three-year-old master plan. The value of Bedford building permits leaped from $4,700,000 in 1970 to $12,900,000 in 1971. The announcements and permits did not change the immediate reality in 1972 that the only restaurant was a Dairy Queen (that subsequently burned) and the only major business was the First State Bank (now First Interstate).

Of the various announced projects only Bedford Forum jelled, and it took far longer than anyone anticipated. Walter Fitch had retired, but his approach toward development continued to prevail until well into the decade. The momentum of the 1960s battle lines persisted. Single-family home construction was readily approved, but councilmen concerned about traffic and congestion hoped to learn from the mistakes of Arlington and Irving; in angrily divided votes they obstructed apartment and commercial zoning and were still slow in providing services. The pie-crust streets were widely criticized, but as one councilman said, "I'd rather have potholes than people." As late as 1973 there were only four apartment complexes in town and four small parks. The population still managed to double in ten years, reaching over 20,800 in 1980. Many in Bedford, as in Hurst, were professionals, Republicans, and northerners escaping the big cities, searching for small town lifestyles.

The price of land in Bedford rose dramatically, in part because, when developers were not allowed to improve their land as intended, they did the next best thing — sell it to the first company that offered them a profit. Some tracts had as many as seven owners between 1965 and 1973. One five-acre tract sold for $37,000 in 1969 and was appraised, still unimproved, by the HEB school district tax office in 1973 for $392,000. Ironically, as the controlled growth advocates temporarily prevailed, residential property prices were speculated out of sight, the land became too expensive for residential development, and unending economic pressure was exerted on behalf of high-density housing and commercial development. Another irony was that the controlled growth champions favored more streets and parks, but the uncommercialized town, virtually devoid of apartments, could not generate enough tax monies to pay for them. It was the inexorable American dilemma for small communities trying to cling to a rural lifestyle in an inevitably suburban locale.

In a 1973 Tarrant County study, UTA Professor of Urban Studies, Paul Geisel, conceded that cities could realize terrific benefits from the sudden tax revenues that new development brought in, apartments in particular, but he contended that in the long term the revenue generated could never match the expenditure that a town had to make to service that development. Concentrated apartment complexes cheapen residential areas, encourage migration, and promote traffic congestion, all of which contribute to the demise of the tax-generating capabilities of the area. Depreciation holds the market value of apartments to a fairly constant level, while the expenditures that a city must make because of the apartments constantly increase. Moreover, the newer complexes attract highly mobile, transient groups who have no more affinity for the community than the apartments' absentee owners. Walter Finch and many other old-line settlers were so determined to preserve their village lifestyle that they truly believed that they could stave off the construction of apartments in the middle of the burgeoning Dallas-Fort Worth metroplex. It was a hopeless ideal. Dr. Geisel knew that apartment complexes could not be avoided, and his demographic studies revealed that if apartments were integrated with residential housing — with a limited number of units per neighborhood, facing the streets, with required landscaping — considerable growth could be accommodated without spawning the usual negative side effects. Such planning, of course, was rare in the metroplex and in the nation, and HEB was typical in isolating apartments along commercial routes.

The Bedford developers argued their cause in elections and eventually prevailed. A crucial factor was the election of L. Don Dodson as mayor in 1972. Backed at the time by Fitch, but not the developers, Dodson ran for mayor in large part because of his cavalier treatment at city hall when he had the temerity to question a proposed development project. Dodson became an effective mediator among the contending factions. Construction in Bedford broke loose in the late 1970s, and stupendous growth lasted into the mid-1980s.

Mayor Dodson had more in mind than allowing some apartments and promoting commercial development. He recalls that "the first thing I did when I became mayor was to go to Dallas and meet with owners of the Boys Ranch property and beg them to sell it to Bedford for a park." By 1974 the mayor had succeeded in getting federal grants to help buy the land and restore the property and float a bond that financed the erection of a new city hall/library complex. The land for Central Park was also acquired. In 1975 builders had to threaten to sue the town to force it to repeal its ordinance requiring builders to pay $125 per new residential water connection (to be used for a city park fund).

In the late 1970s and on through the 1980s neighborhood protests arose when a new six-story hospital, a new water tower, and various apartment complexes were proposed. These efforts generally failed to activate the entire community, but may have had an impact on City Manager Jim Walker's announcement in 1982 that the city was planning too many commercial and apartment developments. If he had any regrets, Mayor Dodson observed in 1986, it was allowing too many apartments, "but that was an evolutionary thing. It happened slowly, almost escaping notice." Actually, much of Bedford's history revolved around the antimerger forces of the 1960s, the controlled growth champions of the 1970s, and the neighborhood protesters of the 1980s. The apartments had been noticed, though Bedford had fewer of them than some neighboring towns. Dodson agreed in 1991 that the net impact of the dissenters probably helped limit apartment construction.

The cycle of the old and the new continued its course. In the spring of 1978, after nearly thirty-three years of active business at 2008 Bedford Road, the Barr and Simmons Grocery Store closed. It began by selling washtubs, wood stove pipes, and kerosene lamps to dairy farmers and cattlemen and ended by selling groceries to airline personnel and other urban professionals. At the same time groundbreaking ceremonies took place for Bedford's first major manufacturing facility, the $3,200,000 Reliance Telecommunications plant. It began by employing about 600 people, about the same number it had in 1991 as the fourth largest employer in HEB.

In 1982 four arts and crafts merchants, seeking to avoid the commercial look and retain the area's authentic cultural flavor, launched the Olde-Town Merchants Society in the former "downtown" area along Bedford Road. Their outdoor craft show began in Gordon Doggett's garage in the early 1970s and peaked in the early and middle 1980s. The Magic Slate was housed in the refurbished Mosier Valley School. The Society foundered, but preservationist-minded citizens were more successful in urging the restoration of the town's only historic structure, the Bedford School Building. Architectural evaluations finally commenced, despite a January 1991 fire. The city established the Bedford Historical Foundation in 1993, chaired by Doggett, to operate the Bedford School Museum and associated shop. The restoration is scheduled for completion in 1994, and the building is presumably the only structure in HEB which may qualify for the prestigious National Registry.

"Through the years Hurst and Euless have outclassed us in salaries, equipment, and personnel," Bedford police and fire fighting officials noted in 1981, but they added that the situation was changing. Bedford still had the lowest taxes and most questionable services. By 1984, however, a municipal service study of 151 Texas cities listed Bedford as one of only fourteen towns to rank in the top 10 percent three times.

In 1971 the Bedford Environmental Design Committee took a reporter on an imaginary voyage of Bedford in 1991. A monorail whisked people around, but many of the city's 55,000 residents walked from their homes through innumerable botanical gardens to their jobs. Symphonies performed at Bedford's Cultural Center across the street from the site of Bedford School, which had been replaced by a recreation hall. A city college was also apparently located in the central business district. None of this came to pass, but in 1994 committees dreamed of a new downtown Bedford, still within the Bedford Road – Airport Freeway area. The new vision — after several permutations — called for 150 acres of waterways,

open air markets, speciality retail shops, office complexes, restaurants, parks, and a publicly financed conference-fine arts center. Many citizens believed in 1971 and 1991 that Bedford was just another suburb that lacked an identity, and that they needed to create a downtown. A crossroads meeting place for Bedford, the most populous of the tri-cities in the early 1990s, would presumably help provide a sense of community and centrality for its 44,000 residents.

In 1994 there was not necessarily any organized opposition against the project but some residents tended to be more worried about immediate problems, such as crime, streets, and traffic, while city officials focused on economic development. Ideally, commercial development boosted the tax base so that cities could cope with immediate problems. Many HEB residents, probably a growing number, believed that they live in a nonplace, perhaps because, as of this printing, there is no centralized city with a well-traveled downtown; the freeways seem to have eliminated the need for it. Bedford (or any of the mid-cities) is their exit off the highway, their access to the airport and the malls, their local school and grocery store, and their own small neighborhood. With the help of considerable citizen advice, however, Bedford's proposed central business district attempted to restore some of the lost ambiance and at the same time create a downtown. It proposed to be less like a congested central city and more like a cultural district/farmers' market.

Possible complications arose when Bedford's politics suddenly took an unexpected turn in November 1991. The city council, in a closed session, voted three-to-two to terminate Jim Walker, the city manager for thirteen years. No reasons were cited, other than Walker's alleged "meddling" in the newly-appointed ethics commission. A month later Councilman Ed Walters labeled Walker's style as "management by intimidation." Mayor Dodson claimed the firing was illegal, and in April 1992, a district court ruled that the lack of a public hearing and written charge constituted a violation of Walker's due process. Walker was reinstated. Meanwhile, Don Dodson, unopposed for nine terms, drew opposition for reelection from former Councilman Leroy Leddon, who was far less keen than Dodson on retaining Walker's services. In a bizarre twist, Dodson retired from office after the filing deadline and subsequently supported the write-in candidacy of airline pilot Rick Barton. Barton defeated Leddon, 1,285 to 1,233. All the instigators of the uprising — labeled by the *Mid-Cities Daily News* as a temporary "city hall orchestrated fracas" — were beaten in the 1991 and 1993 city elections, but they have not given up their desire to overhaul city management.

There was some concern in the early 1990s that either the vacancy rate in Northeast Tarrant County that reached 30 percent or the Walker matter might endanger the development of the central business district. Neither factor, however, immediately attached itself to the "downtown" issue. The greater potential obstacle by 1993 was rising antitax sentiment. At first the city council considered funding the fine arts center in the central business district with anticipated Proposition 15 sales tax money, but backed away. Proposition 15, a half cent sales tax increase, was then earmarked for park and recreation projects, but it was voted down in August 1993 by 2,067 to 929. If the Bedford Taxpayers Cooperative took on the funding of the fine arts center with the same energy and adroitness it used against the proposed sales tax hike, the long awaited birth of the central business district obviously will be hindered. The next relevant balloting occurred in the May 1994 mayoralty race between former city councilman Rick Hurt and political activist Scott Fisher. Hurt was involved in the effort to fire Walker and believed that the city should "get out of the development business."

Euless, meanwhile, has traditionally been governed more loosely than its neighbors. In 1957 W. M. "Blackie" Sustaire became Euless' first city employee when he was hired as chief of police. Thinking he would stay temporarily, Sustaire eventually became city manager in 1974 and retired in 1989. More than any other single person, he set the tone for Euless' government. The zoning codes in the 1960s and 1970s were probably the least strict in the tri-cities, and some questionable projects slipped through. (Euless' zoning laws have also allowed smaller lots and homes than its sister cities, but this was not solely because of city codes. Carr Collins' development set the precedent, and land was simply too expensive at that time to carve into larger pieces.) The hands-off approach was also illustrated by city officials in the 1970s who would not even consult their traffic safety coordinator about traffic flow around a proposed project. By the 1980s the Euless zoning ordinances were similar to those elsewhere, and additional city staff and engineers in the 1980s and

1990s allowed Euless to be more selective in its approach toward development.

After the construction of the town's municipal complex and the purchase of the water and sewer system in the mid-1960s, the anticipated completion of Airport Freeway and the regional airport next door forecast the next key developments. The freeway would put Dallas within easy commuting distance, and the airport would open the metroplex to world commerce. In 1970 the leveling of the old Euless Elementary School on South Main, parts of which dated back to 1913, symbolized the arrival of the new era. City Manager C. J. Griggs proclaimed that Euless had no problems. Even before airport construction was announced in 1972, speculators anticipated a surge in homebuilding and in commercial and industrial development, and they quickly drove land prices out of reach. Slowed also by the high inflation of the early 1970s, Euless' growth suddenly ceased. Only four multifamily building permits were granted in 1972 and none in 1973; only two single-family building permits were issued in 1974. Another problem was that the northeast portion of town, containing most of the undeveloped land, had no major thoroughfare. When Harold Samuels became mayor in 1975, he noted that one key to more commercial and industrial development would be the extension of State Highway 360 North of Airport Freeway. It became a thirteen-year lobbying effort that consumed much of his time, before State Highway Department approval was granted in 1988.

Many tracts reverted back to their original owners by 1979 and growth began to resume, given a considerable boost the next year by the establishment of Euless Town Centre. The population had increased some 24 percent during the decade and numbered 24,000 in 1980. In the early and middle part of the 1980s Softball World opened on Euless Boulevard and was touted as a means of drawing teams from across the nation. The 700-acre residential and commercial complex, Villages of Bear Creek, was launched by a Dallas firm that seemed to hope that Highway 360 would come through at any moment. The city adopted a future land use plan in 1983, something that city officials conceded had been needed for some time. In 1984 for the first time one of the airport enterprises within the Euless city limits was listed as one of the city's top ten taxpayers. Several businesses moved in, such as Atlas Match Company, Caravan Express, White Swan Foods,

Santa Fe Railroad, and K-Mart Regional Headquarters.

The Beautify Euless Everyday Committee formed in 1981, and the city won the governor's "Keep Texas Beautiful" Award in 1982 and 1986. The park system expanded from nine to fourteen facilities, and so many trees were planted and transplanted as part of a new landscaping policy that the city purchased a hydraulic tree spade. The innovative forty-acre Villages of Bear Creek Park won the Texas Urban Forestry Council Award in 1993. The Euless Historical Preservation Committee was established in 1993, with the support of the city, to collect records and photographs and preserve the city's history.

But the years since the mid-1980s have been another difficult period. Neighborhood residents worried about the influx of apartments have protested that the loss of single-family zoning leads to congested streets and a spiraling crime rate. The Villages of Bear Creek developer went bankrupt in 1986. In 1988 a multifaceted bond election failed at the polls. Population growth continued, however, as Euless surpassed 38,000 in the 1990 census.

Euless' commercial growth has been limited, in part because only a short portion of Airport Freeway is within its city limits. And several acres of prime real estate along it are taken up by non-taxpaying entities, Trinity High School, the First Baptist Church, and the city's municipal complex. Moreover, a part of the town's economic development is out of its hands — it is the land at the airport that is within the city boundaries. This includes the east side of Highway 360.

A second negative feature of the airport's location was that the upsurging land values it triggered, as well as the presence of a plethora of small land owners, discouraged hotel building. Hotels seeking sites near the airport settled in Irving, near the airport's north entrance.

A third deleterious effect of the airport became evident in 1988 with the airport's announced decision to alter its master plan, by adding two runways and a westside terminal to its present facilities. It sparked the formation of an active homeowner's group who was outraged by the prospective noise pollution. (Misunderstandings date back at least to 1979 when Paul Spain — at Villages of Bear Creek — announced that airplane noise was going to decrease in the future, and airport deputy executive director Jack Downey announced that the noise would increase, that

development was coming too close to the airport, and that future political and legal problems were being created. Euless' industrial zoning along the edge of the airport had been replaced by apartment zoning.) What no one anticipated was that the airport might change its master plan and argue that expansion was urgently needed to insure the safety of millions of passengers. The loss of some 850 homes, valued at approximately $100 million risked lowering property values in bordering areas and cause a diminution in tax strength across the city. Other residents faced the possibility of having to make up lost tax revenue from homes depreciated or taken by expansion. The D/FW Airport Board through its staff tentatively offered only $25 to $35 million for buyouts in Euless, and the city filed suit in 1991 to halt the expansion.

In October 1991, the 162nd State District Court Judge, Bill Rhea, ruled in favor of Euless, Grapevine, and Irving. The judge held that the cities did not have to allow the expansion, since they controlled zoning within their boundaries. Legal battling continued and by the end of 1992 Euless had spent about $1,500,000 in court cases. Upon convening in January 1993, the state legislature was faced with airport lobbying on behalf of a bill that would give the facility control over land use. Otherwise — as noted by former state representative Charles Evans, an airport lobbyist — American and Delta might have to reroute flights to other cities, wreaking a negative impact on business and industry all over Texas. By the early 1990s nearly two-thirds of all Texas' air cargo was shipped through DFW Airport. While some legislators were wary of trampling on the home rule rights of cities, the lure of an alleged $3.5 billion construction project, 31,000 jobs, and a $30 billion stimulus to the overall economy in the next twenty years proved to be overwhelming. The new 1993 law appeared to give D/FW Airport the authority to build two new runways, but the original state district suit as of 1994 was still on appeal. And the three cities of Euless, Irving, and Grapevine also filed an environmental challenge to runway expansion which was pending in 1994 in a federal court in Washington, D.C.

Euless also lacked the support of Hurst and Bedford, both of which would benefit from increased commercial traffic at the airport. As the *Mid-Cities News* reported, "Both cities boast large numbers of airport and airline employees as residents, including Bedford Mayor Rick Barton, who is an American Airlines pilot." The HEB Chamber of Commerce fully supported expansion (along with an equitable solution) and the American Airlines Training Center at Highway 360 and Airport Freeway was among the ten largest taxpayers for the HEB school district.

The constitutionality of the 1993 state law is being tested. Litigation may drag on for years and may even reach the U.S. Supreme Court. It may be dragged out so long that a new regional airport will be built, as recommended in a 1991 study by the Council of Governments. A new airport would negate the need for a west side (Euless) runway for the old facility. Part of the price and part of the irony of living in a huge urban complex is that seemingly innocent communities sometimes pick up the bill left behind by clashing developers — yet the developers were representative of the communities.

As institutions and traditions such as the Old Settlers' picnic and the Fuller brothers' grocery die off, new ones are born. In 1982 area disk jockey Terry Dorsey developed his comic notion that Hiney Wine was brewed in Euless at a site behind the library and marketed in a flip-top can. Crude Hiney Winery stories were syndicated in scores of radio stations across the country. Dorsey based his original opinion of Euless on a couple of "strip joints" that were actually in Fort Worth, but he continued to use Euless' name in some of the stories and commercials. Prominent citizens such as Mayor Samuels and Reverend Jimmy Draper were not amused, and it appears in the 1990s that the yarn has faded away.

A new tradition more pleasing to city fathers and more representative of the community's spirit, was the annual Leisure Faire, begun in 1989, renamed Arbor Daze in 1992, a reflection of the city's commitment to planting trees. Any profits generated were plowed into the park system. Held in the city municipal complex and funded by several corporations, it has become a three-day extravaganza featuring arts, crafts, lawn and garden shows, and music. The mid-April 1991 event drew some 10,000 people. Attendance in 1992 was estimated at 27,000, and in 1993 at 55,000. Carnival elements were introduced in 1994, as over 80,000 attended.

Perhaps the most newsworthy religious development in HEB has been the rise of Baptist fundamentalism since the 1970s, especially in Euless. The Reverend Jimmy Draper arrived at the First Baptist Church of Euless in 1975 and later served two terms as president of the 14 million-member Southern Baptist Convention. Draper, supported by his 9,000-person congregation, focused some of his message on the inerrancy of the Bible as the guiding light for daily living. At that time he was involved in modern controversies, asserting, for instance, that God opposes abortion, the teaching of evolution, and the federal ban on school prayers. He departed in 1991 to accept the presidency of the Southern Baptist Sunday School Board in Nashville.

Still more conservative in 1994 was the nationally prominent James Robison Evangelistic Association, which began in Euless in 1971. The Reverend Robison was dropped from a metroplex television station in the late 1970s because of a controversial program against homosexuality, but reinstated after 12,000 fans demonstrated their support for him. His ministry began accumulating debts and alienating many fellow Southern Baptists in 1983 when Robison began emphasizing gifts of the spirit, including faith healing and casting out of spiritual demons. His national television ratings plummeted after the televangelist scandals of 1988, but in 1994 the ministry was financially healthy and was building a TV studio on Highway 10 in Euless.

Mid-cities churches boomed along with the towns. A 1990 survey counted forty-three Baptist churches in Northeast Tarrant County, seventeen United Methodist, fifteen Church of Christ, fourteen Assembly of God, and lesser numbers of others. The largest single denomination was Saint Michael's Catholic Church in Bedford, with over 10,000 members. Various studies through the years indicated, however, that the growth rate of the churches was not keeping pace with the growth rate of the towns.

Politico-religious tensions were evident on occasion. In 1989 the Bedford City Council declined to adopt a right-to-life resolution that denounced abortion and the Planned Parenthood Federation. Voices for Educational Rights was established in 1992 when some parents became concerned over allegedly stealthy efforts by ultraconservatives to stymie public education programs about AIDS, drug prevention, and multiculturalism. In June 1993, after an agonizing ten-month study the HEB school trustees approved a guide that stressed sexual abstinence and gave parents the option of exempting their children from lessons that deal with AIDS. But discussions of preventive measures for students who may be sexually active was included in the curriculum. In July 1993 Operation Rescue, the fringe of the anti-abortion movement, held rallies in Metroplex Chapel in Euless. Operation Rescue founder Randall Terry's July 13th speech drew a crowd of over 300, who sympathized with Terry's fervent demand that the U.S. be turned into a "Christian Democratic Republic based on the Ten Commandments." Some Bedford voters were perturbed by the mayoralty candidacy of Scott Fisher in 1994. Fisher at that time was communications director for the Texas Christian Coalition, a branch of controversial Republican Reverend Pat Robertson's political action committee.

HEB has always been heavily Anglo, but minorities began to migrate into the towns for the same opportunities that attracted the Anglos — better schools, housing, and jobs. African Americans, Asians, Hispanics, Tonganese, and American Indians increased some 290 percent in HEB in the 1980s, though they still numbered only about 17,300 out of a total HEB population in 1990 of some 115,500. Northeast Tarrant County's population mirrored the rest of the nation more closely in 1994 than at any time in the past. Institutions slowly adapted to the changes — Bellevue Baptist Church in Hurst, for instance, welcomed all to its fellowships, but divided its congregations into Anglo, African American, Chinese, and Korean.

Mosier Valley, meanwhile, has been neglected by Fort Worth and is in danger of disappearing as a community. Its remaining 150 residents seem overwhelmed by gravel pits and machine shops, and many families rely on well water and septic tanks. In 1994 Mosier Valley was selected for one of Fort Worth's four Target Area Planning programs, which were supposed to promote high visibility improvements. Long-time resident Vada Johnson, a descendant of Mosier Valley pioneers, stated that the new program presents "more hope than we've had."

HEB school enrollment growth stopped abruptly in 1970, and the numbers of students did not change much in the 1970s and 1980s. The usual school board battles were fought over long hair styles and the high pay of athletic directors. Computers were introduced into a few classrooms in 1978 and a program for academically gifted students began in 1980. Changes did not necessarily come easily, however. Upon holding hearings in Bedford in 1984 to determine public opinion on optional preschool programs for four-year-olds and longer school days, the State Board of Educa-

tion was denounced by some conservative HEB parents as fostering socialism. In 1994 the district was proud of its students' stellar performances in recent years on college entrance exams, TAAS tests, and in academic decathlons. The highly-rated PEAK program (Pupils Excelling in Ability and Knowledge) began in 1979, one of the first such programs to receive state funding. With about 2,000 employees, the school district at this time was the largest employer wholly within HEB and one of the twenty-five largest in the county.

The district remains well known for the fervid football rivalry between the L. D. Bell Blue Raiders and the Trinity Trojans. In 1982 the 14-1-1 Blue Raiders met the 12-1-1 Trojans in the state quarterfinals and fought to a 14-14 tie. Their two matches that year drew 62,000 fans at Texas Stadium in Irving. Bell won the tie game on penetrations, then lost in the state playoffs. The playoff earnings put $335,000 into the district's general fund and indirectly led to the building of Pennington Field five years later. The Trojans made it to the playoffs for a decade between the mid-1970s and mid-1980s and to the state finals in 1992.

Tarrant County Junior College's (TCJC) northeast campus became directly involved in the community, offering the usual array of courses for potential transfer to senior colleges as well as such specialized, professional ones as fashion merchandising, real estate, nursing, medical training, and composite bonding classes (teaching a skill required for making the skin that covers Bell's V-22 Osprey). By the time of the 1990 anniversary celebration of its 25th year (since the county vote authorizing its construction), TCJC had enrolled some three hundred thousand students, about half of whom were and are the first in their families to attend college. Half the students take university parallel courses, which are accepted at the University of Texas at Arlington (just twelve miles south of the high schools) and other universities. The Heritage Room in the TCJC Library, along with the Tarrant County Historical Commission, has been instrumental in preserving the area's history. The northeast campus became the site for most of the College for Kids classes, launched with six courses in 1982. By 1992 some 324 three-week-long sections were taught to third through eighth graders interested in summer education, often in subjects not found in most schools, e.g. astronomy and backyard paleontology.

The Trinity Arts Guild moved from Hurst to the revamped Bedford Boys Ranch in 1975. It continued to be a nonprofit association of professionals and amateurs who offered classes in the visual arts and sponsored exhibitions and presentations. Renamed the Northeast Tarrant Arts Council in 1991, it served some 800 people per week in 1994.

Juvenile gangs appeared in HEB in the early 1990s, with an estimated 200 teens involved as of 1992. Violent crimes also increased. HEB police responded with gang task forces, police store fronts, foot and bike patrols, adopt-a-cop programs, drug awareness and youth programs, and video cameras in patrol cars. Police officers were stationed in every school for the first time in 1993. HEB undoubtedly needed more after-school programs, since about half of all students by the sixth grade are home alone or with each other. The expense of remaining open is the main reason schools close in HEB and other metroplex districts. As the *Star-Telegram* noted early in 1994, Tucson, Arizona, expanded its recreational programs after hours in schools for "a modest $400,000 of the city's $47,000,000 budget . . . Volunteers helped the city stretch the dollars with hands-on assistance." Businesses were called upon to develop plans to help deter gangs in Fort Worth and Irving, but in early 1994 businesses were not yet involved in juvenile crime in HEB or Arlington. Some individual businesses, e.g. Putt Putt Golf and Games in Hurst and Showplace Lanes in Euless initiated their own crackdowns. Today violence, gangs, and drugs are additional evidence that the suburbs cannot escape the breakdown of families and schools and other urban phenomena. The challenge for HEB and many other American communities is to control the gangs before they become a menace.

Hurst General Hospital, with twenty-five beds, was founded in 1961 by Drs. Charles Bragg and Virgil Jenkins. The HEB Community Hospital opened in June 1973, with sixty-seven beds and 211 personnel. It promptly crashed — due to a dearth of patients and a rogue computer billing system — forcing the resignation of the hospital administrator. In 1974 the nearly bankrupt hospital affiliated with the Harris Hospital Methodist system. In 1978 it merged with Doctors' Hospital in Euless and claimed 212 beds. Troubles continued, however, when in 1982 several doctors accused it of offering free ambulance services in order to garner more patients. The hospital denied it. Also in 1982 Hurst General and Harris Methodist learned that half the people in Northeast Tar-

rant County went to Fort Worth and Dallas for hospital care. With Glenview Hospital in North Richland Hills, the trio threw $88 million into construction of newer and larger facilities, adding about 600 permanent new jobs. Hurst General outgrew its site at 817 Brown Trail, moved to Airport Freeway in Bedford, and opened as Northeast Community Hospital in July 1983, with 500 beds. Perhaps the best known of its special services is its environmental care unit, one of only a handful in the country. Northeast installed a huge Diagnostic Imaging System in 1992, part of a $7 million improvement plan. Harris Methodist established a cardiac catheterization lab in 1987 and opened the $5 million Edwards Cancer Center in 1990. By then it was licensed for 373 beds. With the new, upgraded facilities the quality of Northeast Tarrant County hospitals approached that of the downtown Fort Worth hospitals.

Still other kinds of treatment were available at other kinds of institutions. The Euless Nursing Center, for instance, founded in 1969 in the countryside (now 901 Civic Drive) in 1994 was the only twenty-four-hour, long-term health care facility for the elderly and convalescents in Euless. Kaiser Permanente, the nation's largest health maintenance organization, expanded to Texas in 1979 and opened an HEB office in 1986. Its Norwood Plaza center handled over 2,100 office visits per month.

As federal assistance programs were cut in the 1980s, private, local charities responded to the growing need for emergency assistance programs. As an affluent area, the northeast was the slowest sector of Tarrant County to react. Fort Worth had more people who walked the streets and were hungry, but the distances that insulated the midcities from downtown poverty also created problems for people who needed the agencies that traditionally located downtown. The *Mid-Cities Daily News* ran a series of articles on HEB poverty in December 1986. The ranks of the poor were growing, especially among young families who had never sought assistance before. The tri-cities had no emergency shelters. The lack of a public transportation system also limited many poor families' ability to receive aid or search for work. Another difficulty was the lack of affordable child care for the large number of single parents, particularly women, who had children and who were sole providers. Over 300 churches, social agencies, and government departments coordinated their efforts daily through Emergency Assistance of Tarrant County, formed in 1980. A few businesses, unions, and schools also contributed to various relief and rehabilitation efforts. Indefatigable caseworker Mari Elledge observed in 1986 that part of the problem was "the unwillingness of people" in the northeastern sector of the county to admit that poverty was a problem.

Much of this attitude was overcome. By 1991 YMCA, Red Cross, NETS (Northeast Transportation System), and other private vehicle services assisted the handicapped and elderly. The United Way and nine other agencies and programs, including a county clinic, concentrated their efforts at 813 Brown Trail in Bedford. A second clinic that accepted Medicaid patients opened in November, 1992, on Bedford-Euless Road. Brooks House opened on Bedford Road in 1991, for runaway and troubled teenagers. North East Emergency Distribution and the Open Hands Center in Hurst tried to keep free lunch programs going while school adjourned in the summers. The Comprehensive Wellness Center in Euless relied on volunteer doctors, social workers and lawyers to cope with the sexually abused. Some community groups were more involved than ever in annual events. UAW locals 317 and 218 and their employer, Bell Helicopter Textron, established their Adopt a Family Partnership Program in 1993, working with the Richland Hills churches' Community Enrichment Center, and provided nearly 300 children with Christmas presents. It became an annual event.

These efforts were effective, although financing was tenuous for some, as illustrated by the inability of some of the agencies to expand to full-time operation. Also, there is still no emergency shelter.

Today, probably the greatest need is for a public transportation system connecting the seventeen towns of Northeast Tarrant County to Dallas and Fort Worth. Only a public transit network can reach far flung job sites or job-interview locations. (Such a network would be facilitated by a thoroughfare plan, which doesn't exist either, because HEB and neighboring Northeast Tarrant County towns never worked in concert to develop one.) A fact of life in many American towns is that auto-oriented suburbs frequently do not have transit systems, and tax money is more readily available for the needs of the elderly, who vote in far greater numbers than the poor.

In 1982 Hurst and Bedford established a senior citizens center at Bedford Boys Ranch, originally a 5,000 square foot facility providing games and exercise and ceramics classes. By 1986 the center had become so popular that a 2,200 square foot addition was added for its 1,200 members.

The only HEB efforts to facilitate transportation dealt with traffic flow and development, especially the proposed extension of State Highway 360 northward through Euless and Grapevine (the service roads were finished in July 1992) and the utilization of Railtran, the old Rock Island tracks owned by Fort Worth and Dallas. The two big cities had done nothing with Railtran and probably conceived of it only as an airport train. HEB would be lucky to wangle a Railtran station, perhaps at Bell Helicopter Textron. In 1993 local congressmen developed a proposal for federal funding, but local, state, and federal budgetary constraints made any transit project unlikely. The tracks roughly parallel old 183, changed to Highway 10 in 1979, an 8.8 mile strip from Loop 820 to Airport Freeway that was by-passed in the 1960s as Greater Southwest Field withered and Airport Freeway was constructed.

Since the early 1980s Hurst and Euless have contemplated the revitalizing of Highway 10 for commercial and industrial development and the widening of the highway to six lanes, which commenced was 1990, is part of that plan. So were tax abatements and multi-use zoning. Some city leaders thought choice businesses could be lured to the old highway with tax incentives, but many commercial real estate brokers and urban planners thought the span, with several blighted spots, was more suitable for light industry and warehouses. Either way, the old main drag, averaging less than 20,000 cars per day in the early 1990s, was likely to see more traffic. By 1993 Airport Freeway handled well over 200,000 cars per day and some motorists were expected to begin avoiding the congestion by using Texas 10. By the early 1990s the heaviest traffic load in the county was the confluence of southbound Texas 121 (where three lanes funneled into one, sometimes backing up traffic over a mile) and the west-bound lanes of Airport Freeway in Bedford. The state planned to widen 121 someday.

By 1974 there were some fifty-seven manufacturing firms inside the corporate limits of HEB. Continental Telephone, with about 400 employees, and ECC Corporation were two of the largest. Most were tucked into new industrial parks like Bell Industrial District, International Regional, Euless Industrial, or Bedford Forum.

With an estimated 42 percent of the HEB labor force, mostly male, commuting outside the city limits, manufacturers such as ECC Corp. employed the women who had been left at home. In 1979 the corporate headquarters of American Airlines moved back to its metroplex birthplace, specifically to the east side of Euless, and soon replaced Bell Helicopter Textron as HEB's largest employer. American's area workforce grew from 4,500 in 1979 to 25,000 in 1990. GTE Directories, established in 1935, relocated its headquarters to Dallas-Fort Worth Airport in 1984. One of the world's largest directory publishers, it employs over 6,000 and sponsors various HEB cultural and entertainment activities.

Other large employers were in the service sector. By 1990 the HEB school district employed almost 2,000 and Harris Methodist Hospital about 1,150. Of Tarrant County's twenty largest facilities in each category in 1990, it was in keeping with HEB's professional image that it had three of the largest secretarial services, three of the largest trade and technical schools, three of the largest engineering firms, four of the largest trade and professional organizations, five of the largest residential real estate firms, and seven of the largest computer retailers.

No sector of the modern U.S. economy is immune to hard times. In the early 1990s not only was Bell Helicopter threatened with loss of contracts, but also real estate, construction, and retailing faltered. The airport announced possible layoffs. And in April 1993, Robert Crandall of American Airlines announced that over a 1,000 jobs would be cut that year. Yet it was also true by the 1990s that HEB and Tarrant County had a diversified employment base and created many of their own jobs.

Many problems, such as flooding, tend to flow across city boundaries. Continued construction through the years along with the building of some apartments and additions on flood plains created problems by the 1970s. Over sixty Bedford homes were subject to occasional flooding from Valley View Branch, and residents complain that Hurst does not always keep the channel cleared upstream. Morrisdale Estates in the southwest corner of Euless was actually built on a flood plain in the mid-1960s and has been victimized by damaging Sulphur Branch floods since the early 1970s. Residents have complained bitterly that upstream Bedford, where most of the water

comes from, has done nothing constructive about the channel and that neither has Hurst or Euless itself. Cooperation among the three was sporadic because voters were reluctant to approve costly drainage projects that were designed to benefit only one neighborhood or citizens in other towns. By 1990 the Corps of Engineers began to examine the Morrisdale problem and the mid-cities began to create drainage utility districts to pay for projects.

Talk of merger in HEB still bubbled over occasionally. In 1971 a Hurst planning panel recommended that HEB combine police, fire fighting and library facilities, but nothing happened. Among ninety-two HEB business and civic leaders surveyed in 1972, two-thirds of the group as a whole favored a merger of the three towns, but the leaders of the city governments opposed it. Most of the leaders believed that voters would not support it. There was considerable community pride in each of the three. Cooperative endeavors were apparent, but so was a competitive spirit. A divisive jealousy plagued the HEB police departments in the 1970s, and the towns occasionally threatened to close streets to restrict each other's development. In 1981 Bart Burnett, who managed the HEB Chamber of Commerce in the 1970s, believed consolidation would occur when it became economically beneficial, as it had for the school districts. "It's ridiculous," he said, "to maintain three police departments in a twenty-square-mile area." In 1986 Professor Geisel bluntly told the Chamber that the towns were wasting "time, money, and energy trying to run themselves as three totally individual cities. . . . There are no geographic boundaries between the cities here — just artificial political lines that sometimes get in the way." By 1991 he suggested the merger of planning boards, with the three town councils retaining veto powers.

Others in the 1980s, however, thought that the rivalry was productive. City officials seemed to be more responsive to their people regarding tax and utility increases when the rates might be lower just across the street. Police and firemen felt the competitive edge and did not like to be outdone, and the water departments tried hard not to run out of water when a neighboring city had plenty. School officials had to deal with two cable television franchises in the cities, but came up with a better classroom system than one franchise could have provided.

In 1981 Hurst Mayor Bill Souder said his city would be reluctant to consolidate because Hurst had already gone through its cost of expansion and had reached a plateau, whereas Bedford and Euless still had much undeveloped land, streets, and drainage. Today, all three are almost built out (except for the west side of some of 360 in Euless) but each still has its separate heritage, its own indebtedness obligations and tax levels, its own political establishment, and a somewhat different orientation within the metroplex. Hurst gets water from Fort Worth and shares a fire cooperative with its big neighbor as well as Bell Helicopter, while Euless gravitates toward Dallas County, where over half of its citizens work. Socioeconomic differences might auger against merger — Euless, for instance, is more of a blue-collar town while Bedford's residents have more management and professional positions. Joint services may be expanded, but a merger seems politically impossible.

Joint efforts invariably succeed, though not always in a textbook perfect process. One of the most recent endeavors began in 1988, when the three towns, the school district, and the Chamber of Commerce joined as equal partners in establishing the Economic Development Foundation, with each putting up $30,000 a year ($30,000 in services in the case of the school district). There were some rocky moments — Mayor Dodson complained in 1990 that Bedford was getting nothing in return, that there were no visible development results after two years and little communication from the board. He wondered why the executive directors of the Chamber of Commerce hired and fired EDF directors instead of the EDF's board. The EDF's last director created an innovative marketing booklet for businesses and a computer system that tracked economic growth, but the cost-conscious cities (represented by the EDF board) terminated the lone paid position in February 1992. Hurst and Euless already had economic development departments by then and Bedford created its own later that year. The contributions

were scaled back to $20,000, but the EDF continued its work.

Growth is not going to solve the financial problems of HEB. Accordingly, in 1991 the Chamber of Commerce revised its action plan to target small business and economic development. Economic development does not just refer to attracting new businesses, but also aiding those already present. Dozens of volunteers with a wide variety of professional expertise, for instance, were available to advise local entrepreneurs. The HEB Chamber adapted to the economic realities of its time and place.

Dallas and Fort Worth grew because of commerce, but suburban areas like the mid-cities were built to provide homes. Commercial services and some manufacturing accompanied this irregular forty-year growth, and the search for smaller businesses continued, but growth for growth's sake was no longer a factor.

HEB's expansion was typical of American suburban growth in that it was too rapid and poorly controlled, and it took its toll on the physical environment and the social fabric. The tax base in all three towns was a continual problem and probably the gravest long-term threat to HEB's future. But the citizens of HEB have adapted, and they seem to have avoided — as well as any American community — the suburban dangers of being mired in conformity without tradition and affluence without style. Suburbia is the essence of the contemporary city, and HEB, in the hub of the metroplex, has come of age.

In the search for the enhancement of the quality of life and the maintenance of a sense of community, it has been vital to preserve a few symbols from the village past. The Bedford School and Bobo's restored well, the old iron bridge in Euless, and the Hurst School and Parker Cemetery in Hurst, among other historic sites, remind us of our basic values and our work ethic and of how far we have come. In this part of the country, to some extent, the old values are the prevailing values. As Robert Crandall noted, "Nowhere else in the United States has the capacity, ability, and drive that we do here."

1964. In a scene reminiscent of World War II, accelerated production schedules were in effect at Bell Helicopter Company during the Vietnam War. Here Hueys, UH-lB and UH-1D models, move down the assembly line in preparation for combat duty in Vietnam. — Courtesy Bell Helicopter

ca. 1970. Bell Helicopter's sprawling plant south of Hurst and its other assembly facilities in Fort Worth and Arlington provided up to 12,000 jobs during the 1970s, when the nation's defense programs brought several large contracts to the company. — Courtesy Bell Helicopter

1992. L. Don Dodson was mayor of Bedford, 1972–1992, during the period of its greatest growth. He retired without a defeat at the polls. He retired from business in 1993, after twenty-four years as president of Lubrical, Inc. He continues to serve on the boards of several health and human services associations and business organizations.

— Courtesy L. Don Dodson

1993. Mayor William D. "Bill" Souder, a descendant of pioneer settlers, has been postmaster of Hurst, 1949–1971, an organizer and director of several banks, and administrator for Congressmen Jim Wright and Pete Geren. He served on the Hurst City Council, 1976–1980, and was elected mayor of Hurst in 1980.

— Courtesy Bill and Dodie Souder

1993. This is a view of the press room at Quick-Way Stampings Inc., of Texas, which specializes in small lot stampings. It is a quality oriented custom job shop which provides low cost tooling and fast deliveries. Some of the short-run stamping techniques used by Quick-Way were developed in the late 1920s and early 1930s. One of the founders of the company in 1960, Stan Wochnik, was one of the early innovators in the industry. Much of the equipment and processes have been upgraded to utilize computer-generated programs and CNC equipment. In 1971 the company was sold to California businessman Al Schoellerman and is presently owned by his children. Located at 902 Heather Drive in Euless, Quick-Way ships stampings all over the nation and occasionally outside the U.S.

— Courtesy Quick-Way
Stampings, Inc.

Above left. *1993. American Airlines, born in the Dallas/Fort Worth area at the dawn of commercial air transportation, remains one of the largest enterprises in the mid-cities. American and other subsidiaries of the AMR Corp. employ about 28,000 in the D/FW area alone. Despite an aviation industry slowdown, American has continued to expand operations at DFW Airport, its major hub, boarding nearly 14.8 million passengers in 1993. American grew from several small lines, including a carrier created by Fort Worth bus line owner Temple Bowen, that were combined in 1930 as American Airways. It became American Airlines in 1934 under longtime chief executive C. R. Smith, whose contributions – and those of other AA employees – are recognized in the new American Airlines C. R. Smith Museum at American's corporate complex near D/FW Airport. The company's first profitable craft, the 1930s Douglas DC-3, is depicted here at the museum. American returned its headquarters to the metroplex in 1979, after forty years in New York City. — Courtesy American Airlines*

Above right. *1993. Informational picketing at the D/FW Airport was a prelude to the Association of Professional Flight Attendants' dramatic five-day strike against American Airlines in November 1993, which was ended by arbitration. The national headquarters for the 21,000-member union is in Euless, and many of its members live in HEB. The flight attendants of American Airlines negotiated their first contract in 1947, and the union successfully challenged age and marital restrictions in the 1960s. The members, some 85 percent of whom are women, founded the APFA as an independent union in 1977.*

— Courtesy Association of Professional Flight Attendants

Right.
1987. United Auto Workers from locals 317 and 218 at Bell Helicopter Textron are lined up to collect strike insurance benefits at their hall, the old Hurst School. In over forty years of company operation there have been only two strikes, 1969 and 1987, and one company lockout, 1984, along with a few, scattered, brief walkouts. The UAW has become more deeply involved in community affairs over the years, not only in contributions to United Way, Goodwill, Shriners, etc., but also in less traditional programs, such as public housing assistance, the designation of Dunbar High as an adopted school, and annual Easter, Halloween, and Christmas programs for children. — Courtesy United Auto Workers

Left.
1988. In just a quarter of a century Tarrant County Junior College has grown from a vision shared by a few citizens to the seventh largest college in Texas. Its Northeast Campus, which opened in 1969 with 2,711 students, occupies 151 areas straddling the Hurst/North Richland Hills border. The President, Dr. Herman Crow, has been at the post since 1975. The most striking architectural feature is the sixty-six-foot clock tower, completed in 1988 on the west side of the Student Center. TCJC offers a wide variety of courses for those seeking to transfer to universities and for those training for entry into the job market. The fall, 1993 enrollment at Northeast Campus was 12,367.

– Courtesy Tarrant County Junior College

1960s. The iron bridge, built in 1889, was first installed across the Trinity River in Arlington, then moved to Euless North Main spanning Little Bear Creek. Increasing auto traffic took its toll on the structure. It was finally disassembled and reconstructed at its present site in South Euless Park in 1976

— Courtesy Weldon Cannon and the Euless Historical Preservation Committee

1992. Left to right are Jimmy Payton, Bill Souder, Marvin Arthur, and Harold Fuller. They represent some of the forty local families who founded First American Savings Bank. Harold Fuller and Jimmy Payton are descendants of Moody Fuller, who settled with his family in the Euless area in 1866. Hurst Mayor Bill Souder's great grandfather was William L. Hurst, who settled here in 1865. Marvin Arthur is a descendant of F. L. Arthur, who came to the Bedford area in 1866. More than 10,000 local residents are customers of four local offices. The bank has assets of over $130 million.

— Courtesy First American Savings Bank

1993. Landmark Bank, the only bank in Euless, opened in June 1985, with nine employees, $4 million, and thirty-two years of experience between its top two leaders. Since 1990 it has been an independent institution owned and operated by local people. All nine of its board members live in the HEB area. A member of the Federal Reserve System, the bank opened its first branch office in Colleyville in February 1994. By the end of 1993 it had assets of over $43 million, a staff of twenty people, and more than 3,000 accounts. — Courtesy Landmark Bank

1993. Amid the suffering caused by the Great Depression of the 1930s, prominent Fort Worth physician Dr. Charles Harris and the North Central Texas Conference of the Methodist Church had visions of providing quality health care and compassion for anyone who needed it. After ten years of planning and building, Methodist Hospital (its original name) opened in Fort Worth. Thus began a long history of community service in seven hospitals, including Harris Methodist HEB on Hospital Parkway in Bedford. As a member of the fully integrated Harris Methodist Health System, the hospital is a complete medical facility that offers a number of special services. Harris Methodist HEB began treating cancer patients in 1990 with its Edwards Cancer Center, dedicated in memory of rancher Kirk Edwards, who left most of his estate to a foundation that would promote the general welfare of North Texans. Harris Methodist HEB has grown from a 67-bed community hospital to a 219-bed full service health care center. — Courtesy Harris Methodist HEB

1993. Photographer Michael McCaddon took this shot for the Mid-Cities News. *Taken from Bedford's Central Drive and Airport Freeway, looking northwest over a mall and shopping area, it is a snapshot of a modern urban landscape. The* Mid-Cities News *traces its origins in the area to 1909 and has been a mainstay in HEB since the 1960s. It is the only newspaper in the area that concentrates solely on local concerns. It also sponsors meetings to bring people from the various mid-cities together. Published twice a week, it chronicles HEB's social, political, and economic events. — Courtesy* Mid-Cities News

1992. Herman J. Smith, former mayor of Hurst, came to Hurst when the HEB area's population was less than 5,000 people. The Herman Smith companies have played a considerable role in the residential and commercial development of the area. Smith was chairman of the board of First American Savings Bank at the time of his death in 1994.

— Courtesy First American Savings Bank

1993. It took from June to September in 1961 for Hurst General Hospital, Northeast Community Hospital's predecessor, to go from ground breaking to surgery. HEB's first hospital, owned by Drs. Charles Bragg and Virgil Jennings, lay on the Hurst-Bedford boundary at 817 Brown Trail. Hurst General went through several additions and several owners before moving into its new facility at 1301 Airport Freeway and changing its name to Northeast Community Hospital in July, 1983. Health Trust bought the hospital in 1987, along with 102 others around the nation, and formed an employee stock-ownership plan, through which employees own part of the company. It is the largest ESOP in the country. Over 300 physicians on staff represent a wide range of specialties and training. The board of trustees is comprised of area citizens and medical staff members. Northeast Community Hospital is a complete medical facility offering a full range of services.

— Courtesy Northeast Community Hospital

Left.
ca. 1992. Mayor Harold Samuels, left, visits with Mrs. W. M. Sustaire and Congressman Pete Geren. Samuels served on the city council and as Mayor Pro Tem for seven years before becoming mayor, 1975–1993. He is owner of Samuels and Associates, a manufacturer's representative of lighting equipment, and is District Director of conservative Republican Congressman Joe Barton's office. Mrs. Sustaire, widow of City Manager Blackie Sustaire, was present for the dedication in her husband's honor of the city's public safety building. Congressman Geren is a conservative Democrat whose district includes the Euless city complex. Barton and Geren represent HEB in the U.S. House of Representatives.
— Courtesy Harold Samuels

1993. North Hills Mall at Loop 820 and Highway 26 in North Richland Hills, developed by Federated Department Stores, opened in 1979 in a peanut and cotton field. A Sanger-Harris store (now Foley's) was the first anchor store, joined later by Mervyn's and Stripling and Cox. With some eighty stores, it is a consumer-friendly regional mall serving twelve cities, including HEB. It has also become a community and entertainment center for the area. The mall is now owned by JNB Property Co. of Chicago. — Courtesy North Hills Mall

Above:
1982. In their 1982 quarterfinal championship game in Irving Stadium, L. D. Bell and Trinity tied 14–14, but Bell advanced on penetrations to the semifinal game. Photographer Scott Threlkeld, commenting on this prize-winning photograph, said, "I have covered the Super Bowl, the Final Four, many pro and college events, a presidential convention, and a papal visit, but none have matched the intensity and heart I witnessed that December night . . . between two high school teams, cross-town rivals, brothers really, locked in combat, playing for bragging rights, playing for The Dream." Childhood friends John Beasley (14) and Randy Barnard (87) sought each other after the game.
           – Courtesy Scott Threlkeld ca. 1982

Left: *1991. Efforts by Bedford preservationists to save the old Bedford School Building, probably erected in 1912, were seemingly dealt a severe blow in the spring of 1991, when fire gutted the historic structure. Restoration will probably be completed, however, in 1995. It is the biggest restoration project in HEB.*

Selected Bibliography

Books

Abstracts of Land Titles. Tarrant County, Texas. Fort Worth: the Fort Worth Genealogical Society, 1969.

Conner, Seymour. *The Peters Colony of Texas*. Austin: Texas State Historical Association, 1959.

Cushman, Evelyn. *Cemeteries of Northeast Tarrant County*. Fort Worth: E. D. Cushman, 1981.

Farber, James. *Fort Worth in the Civil War*. Belton: Peter Bell Press, 1960.

Gage, Duane. *Scenes from the Past: A Mid-Cities Album*. North Richland Hills: Tarrant County Junior College, 1975.

Garrett, Julia Kathryn. *Fort Worth, A Frontier Triumph*. Austin: Encino Press, 1972.

Haar, Charles (ed.). *President's Task Force on Suburban Problems*. Cambridge, Massachusetts: Ballinger Publications, 1974.

History of Texas. Chicago: n. p., 1895.

Jackson, A. T. *Mills of Yesteryear*. El Paso: Texas Western Press, 1971.

Jones, Joe. *D-FW: Regional Growth Influencing Transportation Planning*. Austin: University of Texas Bureau of Business Research, 1965.

Kelly, Barbara (ed.). *Suburbia Re-examined*. Westport, Connecticut: Greenwood Press, 1989.

Knight, Oliver. *Fort Worth: Outpost on the Trinity*. Norman: University of Oklahoma Press, 1953.

Lingeman, Richard. *Small Town America*. New York: G. P. Putnam's Sons, 1980.

Ray, Thelma (comp.). *The History of Birdville*. Fort Worth: n. p., 1965.

Sanders, Leonard. *How Fort Worth Became the Texasmost City, 1849–1920*. Fort Worth: TCU Press, 1973.

Schmelzer, Janet. *Where the West Begins: Fort Worth and Tarrant County*. Chatsworth, California: Windsor Publications, 1985.

Schwartz, Barry (ed.). *The Changing Face of the Suburbs*. Chicago: University of Chicago Press, 1976.

Tarrant County Historical Resources Survey. Fort Worth: Historic Preservation Council for Tarrant County, 1983

Texas Almanac. 1904–1911, 1931, 1936–1937, 1947–1957.

Williams, Mack. *In Old Fort Worth*. Fort Worth: *News-Tribune*, 1977.

Young, Charles (ed.). *Grapevine Area History*. Grapevine: Grapevine Historical Society, 1979.

Interviews

The author interviewed scores of local residents. Several of the clippings files mentioned below contained additional interviews, and dozens of TCJC term papers, conducted in Duane Gage's classes, were based on interviews.

Newspaper Articles and Clippings

Bedford history files and clippings. Bedford Public Library.

——. Dallas Public Library.

——. *Fort Worth Star-Telegram* Collection, University of Texas at Arlington, Special Collections.

——. Tarrant County Historical Commission.

——. Tarrant County Junior College, Heritage Room.

Biographical files. Tarrant County Junior College, Heritage Room.

Bird's Fort file. Tarrant County Historical Commission.

Bulldog. Bedford School Yearbook, 1951–1959.

Cardinal. Euless High School Yearbook, 1948–1950.

Church history files. Tarrant County Junior College, Heritage Room.

"Euless Becomes 30th District," *Texas Power and Light News*, December 1979.

Euless history files and clippings. Dallas Public Library.

——. Euless Public Library.

——. *Fort Worth Star-Telegram* Collection, University of Texas at Arlington, Special Collections.

——. Tarrant County Historical Commission.

——. Tarrant County Junior College, Heritage Room.

Fitch-George, Evelyn. Bedford clippings file.

Fort Worth Star-Telegram, 1909–1993.

Gage, Duane, "Worth Remembering." Series in *Fort Worth Star-Telegram*, 1984–1985.

Grapevine Sun, 1900–1930.

HEB Schools file. Tarrant County Historical Commission.

Hurst history files and clippings. Dallas Public Library.

——. *Fort Worth Star-Telegram* Collection, University of Texas at Arlington, Special Collections.

——. Hurst Public Library.

——. Tarrant County Historical Commission.

——. Tarrant County Junior College, Heritage Room.

McCray, Jane, "Fort Bird." *Sunday Observer*, July 4, 1976.

Mid-Cities Daily News, 1962–1993.

Mosier Valley files and clippings. Tarrant County Historical Commission.

——. Tarrant County Junior College, Heritage Room.

"Much History Revolved Around Peter's Colony." *The Herald*, December 4, 1963.

Rock Products, July 1953 and February 1954.

Souder, Dodie. Hurst notes.

Tarrant County Schools file. Tarrant County Historical Commission.

Texas Historical Marker files. Tarrant County Historical Commission.

——. Tarrant County Junior College, Heritage Room.

Texas Utility News, 1910s–1940s.

Unpublished Printed Materials

Benton, Don. "Sexton Family History," n.d. Manuscript in possession of Evelyn Fitch-George.

Berrong, Verna Elizabeth. "History of Tarrant County from Its Beginnings Until 1875." M.A. thesis, Texas Christian University, Fort Worth, Texas, 1938.

Brown, Earl. "Community Social Analysis of HEB." Fort Worth: Texas Wesleyan College, 1972.

Fuller, Betty. "Education in Euless," n.d. Manuscript in possession of Fuller.

Gage, Duane. "History of Northeast Tarrant County," n.d. Manuscript in possession of Gage.

HEB Chamber of Commerce. Minutes, 1952–1991.

Holden, Glenn M. "A Partial History of Education in Tarrant County." M.A. thesis, Texas Christian University, Fort Worth, Texas, 1931.

Nott, Frank. "The Bedford-Euless Merger Proposal of 1967," 1991. Bedford-Euless file, Bedford Public Library.

Patterson, Michael. "The Spring Garden Community of Tarrant County," 1981. Bedford history files and clippings, Bedford Public Library.

_____. "William Letchworth Hurst," 1980. Hurst history files and clippings, Hurst Public Library.

Rock Island Railroad Collection. Southern Methodist University, DeGolyer Library.

"Some Background on the Bear Creek Area of Tarrant County." Euless history files and clippings, Euless Public Library.

Wheat, Jim. "Postmasters and Post Offices of Texas, 1846–1930." Compiled from National Archives, Dallas Public Library.

Index